"Amy Young surveyed nearly 200 abroad. *Getting Started* is rich with the challenges, and celebration of the joys from those who have gone before. An essential resource for newbie expats in preparing for an international move."

Rachel Pieh Jones
author of *Stronger than Death and Finding Home*

"Every person's first year of transitioning abroad is challenging, full of unexpected cultural, emotional, interpersonal, and spiritual navigation. While it is easy to question your 'fit' for the field, Amy's storytelling and research in *Getting Started* will affirm that you are EXACTLY where you are supposed to be. Allow Amy to comfort you with her entertaining experiences and her refreshing honesty!"

Lauren Pinkston
Cofounder of *Wearthy*

"If you don't like learning from folks who've gone before you, you probably shouldn't read *Getting Started*. But if you want to learn a ton of crucial lessons from an experienced trainer and transition coach (and the hundreds of cross-cultural workers she interviewed), read *Getting Started*!"

Jonathan Trotter
author of *Serving Well*

"What a delight to read the words of Amy Young in her latest contribution to a growing library of books! In *Getting Started*, Amy offers both the newcomer and the seasoned cross-cultural worker a gift of wisdom, insight, and practical tips to accompany them on this sometimes hard, often times crazy, and always grace-filled journey of cross-cultural work. Her words at the end of the book 'Firsts are special, and this first year on the field will remain with you long after it ends.' is also true of the words of this book. Amy's words will remain with you long after the book ends. I am so grateful for this writer!"

Marilyn Gardner
Author of *Between Worlds: Essays on Culture and Belonging* and *Worlds Apart: A Third Culture Kid's Journey*

"*Getting Started* is a must-have guide for your first year on the field. Drawing from personal experience and collective wisdom, Amy Young shares everything you need to know to thrive."

Dorette Skinner
author of *A Story of Pregnancy and Faith*

Getting Started

MAKING THE MOST OF YOUR FIRST YEAR IN CROSS-CULTURAL SERVICE

AMY YOUNG

Getting Started: Making the Most of Your First Year in Cross-Cultural Service
By Amy Young
© 2019 Amy Young

All rights reserved. Printed in the United States of America. No part of this publication may be reproduced, stored in a retrieval system or transmitted in any form or by any means, electronic, mechanical, photocopying, recording or otherwise, without the written permission of the publisher.

Edited by Deb Hall
Cover and Interior book design by Vanessa Mendozzi

ISBN: 9781089567516

All scripture quotations, unless otherwise indicated, are taken from the Holy Bible, New International Version®, NIV®. Copyright © 1973, 1978, 1984, 2011 by Biblica, Inc.™ Used by permission of Zondervan. All rights reserved worldwide, www.zondervan.com. The "NIV" and "New International Version" are trademarks registered in the United States Patent and Trademark Office by Biblica, Inc.™

Scripture quotations from *The Message*. Copyright © by Eugene H. Peterson 1993, 1994, 1995, 1996, 2000, 2001, 2002. Used by permission of Tyndale House Publishers, Inc.

Scripture quotations marked (NLT) are taken from the Holy Bible, New Living Translation, copyright ©1996, 2004, 2007, 2013 by Tyndale House Foundation. Used by permission of Tyndale House Publishers, Inc., Carol Stream, Illinois 60188. All rights reserved.

Dedicated to
Erin
I am blessed that you were
my first teammate.
You set the bar high
for all those who followed you.

Contents

Introduction — 1

1. Before You Go — 13
2. Somewhere Between Awful and Amazing — 35
3. Welcome to You — 57
4. You Will Be Too (Something) — 75
5. Torn Between Worlds — 93
6. God and You — 113
7. New Relationships (But Not with People) — 125
8. Four Languages You Didn't Know You'd Learn — 143
9. Culture and Team (Finally!) — 167
Conclusion — 183

Acknowledgements — 191
About the Author — 195

Introduction

"I arrived at field orientation yesterday. It wasn't as hard saying goodbye to Mom and Dad as I thought it would be, even though it was Mom's birthday." Thus begins the journal I kept my first year on the field. The entry is fairly short, a paragraph at most, and lacks emotion. I find it interesting the first thing I wrote was related to expectations and my relief that one of 5,437 hurdles I needed to clear to get to the field—the last goodbye at the airport—was less painful than anticipated.

In fairness to me, I was twenty-seven, it was the pre-internet era, and beginning my two-year commitment in cross-cultural service felt like one big adventure. Not an adventure in the sense of being a tourist, exposed to the exotic, but more in the sense of "Finally! Finally I'm here." My "here" had begun five years before in the basement cafeteria of my college dormitory. I was a senior in college who lived on campus for two reasons. One, as a resident assistant it was my job. And two, I thought I would live the rest of my life in "normal" housing, so why not live communally as long as I could. (This will not be the only time you hear angelic laughter; I'm sure you've got your own angels chuckling over you.)

A group from my floor ate dinner together most nights, and early in the school year we had the normal chitchat around "What's your major?" One student said, "Well, my major is engineering but my TOEFL score wasn't high enough, so I have to take ESL classes this semester."[1]

"Oh, what's ESL?" I asked as I ate my meal, ignoring the fact I had no idea what a TOEFL score was.

"English as a Second Language. Even though I studied English in Indonesia for eight years, my English is not good enough to take classes in my major. Hopefully next semester I can start on my real major." And the conversation went on.

Internally, however, I was at a standstill. From that casual comment, I was part confused and part exhilarated. Confused because as an education major why had I never heard of ESL? Why was I hearing about it in a basement over pasta? Exhilarated because God said, "This, Amy, is what you are going to do." And like that, my call to the field was settled. I would teach English in Asia to do my part for the Great Commission. I remember having great peace because teaching was something I could do. Teaching fit me so much better than being on a drama team, working with puppets, singing on stage, or translating the Bible— all things a cross-cultural worker did, according to my limited understanding.

Yet I became disoriented again as I thought, "But how will I be Teacher of the Year in America when I'm teaching in China?" Ah, yes, friend, that was my thought. More about my own glory than lost souls. But it is true, I wondered how I could advance my own career and the Kingdom of God.

---

[1] The TOEFL (Test of English as a Foreign Language) is the standardized test international students take to prove to American colleges that they have adequate language ability to function on a US campus.

INTRODUCTION

At that time, I did not have clear marching orders from God other than "Teach English in Asia," so later that year I attended a large conference for people considering cross-cultural service. I went into the conference with two prayer requests. "God, you know me and you know Asia. Let me know which country and I'll go, and lead me to an organization." In His faithfulness He did, and with a wink at reminding me who was in charge, He added in a few more details.

One of the details was that I needed to earn an MA in Teaching English as a Second Language. Five years would pass between the conference and the journal entry about saying goodbye to my parents. In that time, I earned an MA, spent two summers in China helping with an intensive language training for public school teachers, fell in love with China, recovered from an exhausting ministry experience, and had what I later deemed "the only normal period in my adulthood." For two years I had a job, a roommate, and a lease on an apartment. A life I thought I would be returning to.

That was my path to the field. Maybe what got you "here"—your first year—has been building for months, even years. Regardless, welcome.

Invisible Braces and You

Early on in life, it was evident that I would need braces. Thanks to what my dentist called a "mature mouth," I was the trailblazer in my elementary school as the first person to get braces. The summer between fourth and fifth grade, in preparation for braces I was scheduled to have two permanent teeth removed, creating more space for my existing teeth. As I recall, Mom signed me in at the dental office, made sure all was well, and then ran on a few errands. What I recall in more vivid detail is the actual procedure. I am fairly certain that permanent teeth removal these days will not come with the memories I have . . . because a patient would be knocked out or at least be given laughing gas. Instead, after multiple injections of medication to numb my mouth, the dentist and his assistant went to work on a very-much-awake child.

Dr. Hitch latched on to a tooth, pulling it from side to side. My head was dragged to the left and then to the right, back and forth, as he willed the root to give way. Eventually, he won the tug-of-war and the crack of the root could be heard by all. Or maybe not, but it sure was heard by me. I remember feeling so helpless and trapped and mad. Boy, was I mad. I can't remember if it was after he pulled out the first tooth or the second, but I bit him with all I had. Chances are, my bite was not all that vicious, but Dr. Hitch told me to stop biting him.

Fast-forward more than thirty years and after many moons of enjoying fairly straight teeth, one of my bottom front teeth decided to pop out of line. It poked into my mouth and annoyingly my tongue kept catching on it. What in the world was going on? A few weeks later, as my teeth were being cleaned, I asked my dentist—not my childhood tormentor—why, after decades of having well-behaved teeth, had my bottom teeth started shifting?

He responded as if "everyone knows" that middle-aged teeth move. Well, everyone does not know this. I did not know. One week later I was in an orthodontist's chair having another surreally cheerful conversation about how "everyone knows" middle-aged teeth and gums shift. No one seemed

INTRODUCTION

alarmed or shocked or remotely distressed about my situation, which was a mixture of comfort and annoyance. Shouldn't something this irritating and unexpected elicit a stronger response than I was receiving? Oh well, this wasn't my first rodeo with braces; I knew what to expect.

Or so I thought.

I'm a leaper, not a looker, and I find that information gets in the way of making decisions. The orthodontist showed me on X-rays that the roots of my front bottom teeth had all started to shift, not just the one rogue tooth. I was experiencing the beginning of a "great migration" in my mouth. I did the mental math and planned to have my teeth for years to come and not to have my tongue impaled on shards (aka teeth). So I said, "Yes," to invisible braces.

If you are not familiar with invisible braces, they are plastic trays that snap on and off to holders glued to a few teeth. According to one orthodontist's website, "The comfortable, clear and nearly invisible trays, called aligners, work by using controlled and timed force to gradually move teeth into position. The movement in each patient's case is mapped out by the orthodontist so that each set of aligners move a few teeth at a time. Over the course of the entire treatment, the patient receives a new set of aligners about every two weeks. For most adults, the entire course of treatment is about a year."[2]

You might be wondering why so much talk about teeth in a book about your first year on the field. The idea for this

---

[2] Dr. Patricia Panucci, "How Does Invisalign Move Teeth," Beach Braces, published May 17, 2018, updated July 8, 2019, https://www.beachbraces.org/invisalign-move-teeth.

book started swirling around in my head via a throwaway comment from my group mate Lisa. Lisa and I were in an online small group through Velvet Ashes. Weekly we met with five other women to connect with others who understand this life of cross-cultural service. Lisa had recently returned to the field from time in her home country, and while in the United States had purchased enough Bible studies to last until the next time she was back. She casually commented how in her first year she hadn't realized how responsible she would be for her own spiritual feeding.

Her comment has stuck with me ever since. Every year on the field is unique and special, but like other "firsts" in life, your first year on the field is often in a category unto itself. When I started to coax this book to life, I got nowhere. *Please come out and show yourself*, I would whisper. *But I don't want to*, it would reply. No amount of begging, threatening, or trying to entice these ideas to organize themselves worked.

So, I quit asking and moved on to other projects.

Back to braces. I started wearing invisible ones the recommended twenty-two hours a day. As advertised, the treatment plan was specifically geared to my mouth. At week one, a dental assistant showed me on the computer screen what my mouth looked like on week one. She moved her cursor along the bottom showing week-by-week how my teeth would move and landed on the final goal. Wow, I was impressed! Because I wanted to invest as little time as possible revisiting the pain of my early adolescent experience, I also bought a mouth vibrator. Biting on the device for five minutes a day would decrease by half the time it would take my teeth to move. Sign me up for that! Half the time? I could picture

INTRODUCTION

my rogue tooth back in place.

Wearing invisible braces—I am still in them—is one gigantic metaphor for moving to the field. I knew what I was getting myself into with braces, and yet I was clueless. How could I not be? It is one thing to sit in an office *talking* about what is going to happen, and another to find out I would have a slight speech impediment when I wear the trays.

Because the braces are mostly invisible, I am the primary person to be aware that change is occurring. Of course, friends and family who know I have them ask how it is going, what week I am in, how much longer I have, and what I think about the process, so the fact that my teeth are changing isn't a secret. But the goal of wearing invisible braces is for change to occur, and let's be honest, who is going to be the most aware of those changes? I am waving my raised hand at you emphatically, like a student trying to get the teacher's attention. Me. Me. ME!!!

The mouth vibrator has indeed sped up the process, but it has not removed the reality that there is a process and that change takes time. For a while, I was using the vibrator more than the required five minutes a day hoping that I could radically reduce the time required for change. If you ever find yourself in the same position, I'll share this pearl of wisdom: only do the five minutes. Don't confuse catalysts with shortcuts. You still have to put in the time.

Because I have a slight overbite, I wear rubber bands that are (slowly) training my jaw to have a new resting place. During my week-twenty-five appointment, Dr. River tested my jaw muscles to see how much they had moved. I passed, and he was pleased that the muscles had settled in a different place. Since I like to do well on tests, I was pleased too. But then moments later he wanted to recheck, and my love of looking better than the reality showed her true side. Sure enough, when forced into a natural resting place and not allowed to perform with the idea of where the jaw muscles "should" be, I didn't pass. I still needed to wear rubber bands. It's the same on the field: as time goes by, you will have an idea about where you "should" be when it comes to adjusting to the language, culture, work, and relationships, but you may not get there as quickly as you thought you should. This book is designed to help you begin to release the "shoulds" and allow yourself to be wherever you are in the process of adjusting to the field.

When we talk about the first year on the field, there is nothing magical about twelve months. Your "first year" may in reality last eight or eighteen months. Just like invisible braces are personally designed, God has personally designed your experience. My invisible braces came in three shoe-sized boxes. I counted out the weeks in my head and figured I should be done around Christmastime. Woot, woot! This process was going to take less than a year.

Oh, the assumptions we make about change. If you were getting invisible braces, wouldn't you think that if you were handed two large bags containing your trays and other accoutrements, you would have all you needed at the beginning? I know I did. I did not realize I had made so many assumptions about the process until around week twenty-five when I was in for a routine check and Dr. River made an offhand comment about the next set of trays after week thirty-three. For his sake, I'm glad his hands were far away from my mouth.

INTRODUCTION

I might have bitten my second dentist.

More than thirty-three weeks? My heart sank. This is a classic example of the curse of knowledge: when you know something, it is hard to remember what it is like not to know it.[3] Dr. River and the dental hygienists all knew I was on the first round of the trays, and because it was obvious to them, they forgot it was not obvious to me. I was holding on to a number that was never the goal.

But guess what? Change is happening. The rogue tooth is no longer out of place, and though I am not at the end of the process, I can see how my mouth has changed for years to come. I do not know what your first year holds. But this I know: you are going to change. And that is one of the goals, isn't it? You are going to the field in part to bring spiritual freedom, to learn to live in a foreign place, to see God at work in and through you. Ultimately to see captives set free and grow in their faith and understanding of the triune God. But in the process you will see evidence of your own transformation as well.

Your first year on the field, you know what you are getting yourself into, and yet how can you fully know? You are joining a large cloud of witnesses who have gone before you and welcome you to the field. My first year was one of the best years of my life. The school I taught at provided housing for my teammate and me. But the school used our apartments to house summer teachers from North America so we couldn't stay after school ended. So that first summer I decided to return

---

[3] Chip Heath and Dan Heath, Made to Stick: *Why Some Ideas Survive and Others Die* (New York: Random House, 2010.)

to the US. During the visit my sister Elizabeth said, "Amy, you haven't said much about China. From your letters you seemed really happy, so why aren't you talking about it?"

"I'm concerned that if I let people know how wonderful it is, you will all want to move to China and then I would lose my support base. Who will support me if you all move to China?" I confessed.

Sidestepping the obvious scarcity mentality here, my sister laughed out loud and said, "Um, I do not think you need to worry about that."

While I will share some of my first year in this book, I know that my experience is just that, my experience. Some of you will have fantastic first years. Unfortunately, after working with hundreds of people over the years, helping them transition to and from the field, I also know that having a fantastic first year is not a given. If you have one, great (it sure is more fun than the alternative), but if you don't, that's okay, it doesn't mean you have "done it wrong."

Getting the Lay of the Land

A word about the first chapter before we begin. Chapter 1 shares predictions several cross-cultural workers made before they set foot on the field. The predictions come from a survey taken by 184 cross-cultural workers, but you will not learn more about the survey until the second chapter. As you read through the first chapter, you might feel confused and want to know more about the survey. My friend Joann says that one

INTRODUCTION

of the keys to success on the field is to "tolerate ambiguity."[4] So you might as well start now.

(I promise, you will not have to tolerate the ambiguity for long!)

---

[4] Joann Pittman, "Living Well Where You Don't Belong," Outside-In, October 19, 2012, https://joannpittman.com/cultural-adjustment/2012/living-well-where-you-dont-belong-full-version.

1
Before You Go

Your first year starts while you are still in your passport country. It begins in your mind as you picture yourself riding a bike, taking public transportation, or walking a long dusty road. You see yourself eating local food, speaking the language, even praying in a foreign tongue. But when you arrive, reality may not seem as idyllic. Instead of channeling your inner Mother Teresa, you make a faux pas, or you need stitches at the local hospital, or you do not like your teammates. In the liminal space between dreams and reality, your journey has already started, so this is where we start.

Care to Predict?
"What do you know about Chengdu?" my friend Kenta asked me. "That I am going to live there," I responded. Kenta and I met as students at the wonderful University of Kansas. He was from Japan and I was from Colorado. Though I had spent two summers in China, only one of us knew what it was like to move to another country. Teach In China (TIC) sent me a handbook about the school I was assigned to teach at. It had been compiled by previous teams and updated each year by the current team at the school. I had looked through the handbook, paying special attention to the description of my

future living arrangements, and skimmed through the rest, which was primarily a history of Sichuan province and the names of the rivers that ran through it.

Looking annoyed at my approach to moving to a foreign country, Kenta stood up from the couch and left, saying, "I'll be back soon." About two hours later he returned and thrust a stack of photocopied pages at me. In his disgust with my lack of knowing anything about Chengdu, he had marched to the library and researched my future home. I thanked him but thought, *Wow, we are really different*, because I knew I wouldn't read what I was holding.

This is not the first time I leaped and only later wondered why in the world I had thought so little about a decision. Prior to moving to China, I did put pieces into place. I added my parents to my checking account and gave them power of attorney. The banking assistant who helped us did not find it humorous when I joked about how my parents now had control of my organs. I was young and thick into the adventure I was about to embark on. *Come on, laugh a little, lady.*

But other realities of life never occurred to me.

I arrived on the field without a single recipe. These were the days before the internet. I guess I assumed I would channel my inner Julia Child and, voilà, know how to cook. Turns out, my inner Julia knew how to slice a potato and fry it. My teammate and I also found peanut butter the consistency of paste and globbed it onto steamed buns for "sandwiches." Beggars can't be choosers. The only Chinese food word I knew when I arrived was *jiaozi*, dumplings, and my journal faithfully records every meal we ate out the first few months. Want to know what we ate at every meal? *Jiaozi*.

Except when our friend Mark was with us. Mark taught at our school the year before and now was studying Sichuan Opera. He spoke Chinese!!! (That simple fact is actually worth twenty-seven exclamation points, but I'm limiting myself to three.) Every meal we ate with him is also lovingly recorded because it was not fried potatoes, pasty PB on a steamed bun, or *jiaozi*. Without Mark, here was my journal entry: "Had fried potatoes for dinner and warmed bread! Who knew they could taste so delicious?" With Mark, we ate chicken and peanuts, twice-fried green beans, and the best eggplant dish on the planet.

 To this day it is a mystery why I moved around the world without thinking about cooking in a foreign land. Especially since I used recipes when I cooked in America. My lack of preparation for food reveals unexplored expectations I had about my first year—albeit embarrassing ones to admit now. Expectations are a large part of your preparation for the field. Several of the questions on the survey I conducted related to expectations. For example, "Before you went to the field, what did you anticipate being hard or challenging parts of your first year?" and "Before you went to the field, what did you anticipate with excitement about your life on the field?"

 Expectations can be sneaky because we often don't know we have them until they are unmet. I expected food to be easy, though I did not realize I expected this until after I arrived in Chengdu. Two veteran TIC teachers were passing through town and stopped to see how the newbies were doing. They offered to walk us through the open market nearby, which sounded like a good idea until it turned out to be overwhelming and disturbing. The meat hung on hooks, and no matter how many times the sellers swatted, the flies kept landing on the meat. It took three months until Erin and I could bring ourselves to buy meat. Thus, all of the potatoes and apples, another staple of our survival diet.

When I think of expectations, it reminds me of seeing prairie dogs. Walking by a field near my home in Denver, I am unlikely to notice how many prairie dog holes there are until "Surprise!" up pops a prairie dog. This is not the best analogy for expectations because I love seeing prairie dogs pop up. But some gaps between expectations and reality are like sighting a prairie dog: delightful. But others? Startling. More like a snake sticking its slithery head out of the hole and scaring my pants off.

I assumed I was going to China for two years, so my expectations were primarily about missing family, sporting events, and holidays. It is hard to believe in this day and age, yet at the time (1995) TIC did not emphasize learning Chinese. The attitude, at least what I picked up on, was, "Hey, learn what you can, but you came to teach English and share hope. Trust that God will open doors." Nowadays, the message TIC sends is quite different. Actually, as I'm writing this, I realize I did have expectations around language. In high school I learned German (though "learn" is a rather optimistic view of what I accomplished). In college I planned to be a Russian major, but after a solid year of busting my butt to get a C in the class, I assumed I was bad at languages. So, combining the message from TIC with the messages from my past, I figured I would fail so it wasn't worth my time.

Given my own cluelessness about my expectations, I was curious if others gave more thought to the challenges that lay before them. Like me, some people responded to the survey with thoughts like "Actually I didn't even think about expectations I had. I was young and foolish, I guess" and "Both my husband and I had grown up in cross-cultural work and I think one mistake we made was thinking it would not be very hard to adjust." However, these folks were in the minority; most anticipated hard or challenging aspects in the first year.

As I analyzed the data from the survey, the responses fall into seven categories: Learning Language and Culture, Missing Family and Holidays, Team Life, Daily Life, The Weather, Aspects of Life Related to Ministry or Job, and the broad miscellaneous category of Other Anticipated Challenges. The top two most referenced areas were related to learning language and culture and missing family and holidays. Out of the 184 responses, 77 specifically mentioned learning the language (42 percent) and 60 referenced a cultural aspect (53 percent) as what they predicted would be the hardest part of their first year. Exactly one-third, 59 of the 184 participants, anticipated missing people and holidays would be the hardest part of moving overseas. As you will see when you read through a sample of the responses, because the question was open-ended, some responses mentioned only one area, while others reported several areas within the same answer.

Without editorial interruption from me (although some responses have been edited for grammatical consistency), here are several responses that give you a flavor of what hardships people anticipated related to the challenges of Learning Language and Culture, Missing Family and Holidays, Team Life, Daily Life, The Weather, Aspects of Life Related to Ministry or Job, and Other Anticipated Challenges:

Learning Language and Culture

"Two areas come to mind when I think about challenges I expected: being back in school regularly (language class) and being here with a husband (first time living overseas I was single)."

"We only anticipated learning the language to be hard. We were so full of passion we truly thought we'd experience very little 'shock.'"

"I assumed language school and learning Arabic at the age of fifty-seven would be hard."

"My top concerns were language, our kids making friends, missing family and comforts of home, and figuring out the culture and new rhythms."

"I knew that it would be a challenge adjusting to living in a culture where I couldn't even read, let alone speak, the language. I expected the challenge of being a single woman in a Muslim culture. I expected to have to learn new ways of interacting and getting around. (I'd never really taxied anywhere before moving on the field!)"

Missing Family and Holidays

"I expected being away from family, especially cousins, to be hard. As well as living in a city and our daughter going to school every day."

"Missing family—being single, so on my own, so to speak—and not knowing the language, even though my ministry was in English."

"Distance from our adult children."

"Holidays away from 'home.' I'm a fairly traditional person when it comes to holidays. Every Thanksgiving and Christmas had looked almost exactly the same for thirty years."

"Holidays with strangers, wondering if my boyfriend and I would make it (we didn't, thank God, but that's not how it felt back then), not knowing the language, wondering if I would get along with my teammates/if they would all be weirdos (they weren't)."

Team Life

"Missing family, developing healthy team relationships."

"I anticipated the challenges of the isolation of our placement. As well as the challenge of becoming a team with two people I had never met before. Two people who were proficient (sort of) in the national language. Two people who were transferring from other areas of the country. Here was me coming in fresh from the US. No language. They both had years of experience with the country. What was I bringing to the party?"

"I wondered how hard it would be to develop healthy team relationships."

"I thought I would struggle with homesickness, cultural acquisition, language learning, transition, and team dynamics."

"Language learning. Adjusting to team. Learning to cook—I was useless."

Daily Life

"I am a very picky eater and very introverted. So, a community culture like Uganda made me nervous."

"Not having local friends."

"Navigating rural roads that I had never driven before, and just driving in general. Finding a curriculum to teach at rural Bible studies that I started. I anticipated that the challenges figuring out adulthood as an expat in sub-Saharan Africa would be intensified. I was twenty-two when I moved."

"I anticipated that I would miss home, miss friends and family, and I would miss the nice, easily accessible food. I knew that things would be different in a way that I would have to learn to live with and not change."

"Language and culture barriers, compound life, demanding work at the hospital, limited places to go/limited food options in the dry season."

The Weather

"I imagined the heat and the living in a polluted massive city. We just knew clearly that God was bringing us there."

"The heat, the language, and the work."

"Missing my parents back home and adjusting to a tropical climate."

"Language, isolation, and cold winters."

"Language, our twin babies, culture, weather—extreme humidity and heat."

"Missing family/friends. Giving up Chick-fil-A and American steak houses. Living with winter six months out of the year."

Aspects of Life Related to Ministry or Job

"Not speaking any Turkish, high work demands, not knowing a soul where I was moving to."

"Language learning, learning the culture, living in close

community with an expat team, not understanding church (language difficulty), challenges of dealing with so much suffering and death in my medical Christian work."

"Learning Arabic, being focused on one thing (Arabic school) after a life in work where I traveled quite a bit and had many diverse things in my life. It was hard, but it was also 'the job,' as our team leader reminded us."

"Lack of articulation of what my role would be."

"Finding a new routine and finding my niche. Seeing any tangible spiritual fruit."

"Culture change. Returning to teaching school, a job I have always loved but hadn't done in quite a few years. We went to Afghanistan; moving to a war zone was a first for us and initially caused apprehension."

"Language barrier, general stress of the trauma work I'd be doing, homesickness."

Other Anticipated Challenges

"I anticipated it being hard to experience the poverty around me."

"Leaving parents, children, and grandchildren behind. Learning a new job after being in the same workplace just short of twenty-five years. Trusting God to provide after a lifetime of regular employment and a paycheck."

"I was concerned with how our kids, ages four and six, would adjust. I worried if they would be safe, healthy, and happy."

"The language, the living conditions, and the traffic. I was terrified of getting ill, although I didn't get ill at all that first year."

"Communicating with supporters."

"Loneliness."

"I anticipated language learning to have its frustrations. I expected motherhood to be a bit of an adjustment. I just underestimated how much!"

Even Jesus Foresaw the Challenges

Two months after arriving in China we took a ten-hour train ride to visit TIC teachers for the National Day holiday—a holiday celebrating Chairman Mao's declaring the founding of the People's Republic of China. Since these teachers were in their second year in China, they had it all figured out—at least that's what it seemed like to me. I about fell over when we ate "real" food. The scales fell off my eyes as I realized, *Wait, we could actually eat like this . . . here?! Who knew!* Miracle of miracles, they had a cookbook. Not just any cookbook, but one published by Wycliffe with recipes designed for people in remote areas. With delight we fanned through the pages and saw recipes for things that you can buy off the shelf in the

GETTING STARTED

US. *Wait, you can make marshmallows, tortillas, and pancake syrup?*

The cookbook included makeshift recipes for things that are hard to get abroad, like sour cream and buttermilk. It also suggested ingredients if you don't have specific ingredients listed in a recipe. Erin, my teammate, and I poured over the pages, selecting recipes we thought we could make, and hand-copied twenty recipes. When we returned to our apartment in Chengdu, we lovingly recopied them once more onto recipe cards, and made our own recipe book by placing them into plastic sleeves inside a photo album.

The survey results highlight that thinking about what might be challenging or hard is universal. Even Jesus thought about the cup sent before him, asking God if He was willing to remove it (Luke 22:42). Part of being human is the ability to look ahead. Jesus was not chastised by God when He mentioned the difficulties before Him and His desire to avoid them. He was not just told, "Trust me!" Instead, Jesus's words are recorded, humanizing and honoring not only His but also our own ability to anticipate challenges before us.

What you predict to be challenging might fall in one of these six larger buckets—Learning Language and Culture, Missing Family and Holidays, Team Life, Daily Life, The Weather, Aspects of Life Related to Ministry or Job, and Other Anticipated Challenges—or it might be more specific and unique. When it comes to what may seem hard or challenging to you, know that you are not alone. Unfortunately, based on the data, I hate to break it to you, but you are probably wrong. People are not as accurate in their predictions as you might guess.

The Language of Anticipation

I first saw the Hallmark movie *Sarah, Plain and Tall* two years after I was called to serve abroad and one year after I attended the cross-cultural conference I mentioned earlier. So when I saw *Sarah, Plain and Tall*, I was in that magical and murky place between being called and being commissioned. I connected with Sarah as I watched the movie. Sarah lived in Maine with her brother who was about to be married, and she also wanted her life to experience a change. A Kansas widower placed an ad in an eastern newspaper for a wife to help him raise his young son and daughter. She replied with the news of her brother upcoming marriage and she need for a change, explaining that "my choice, as you can see is limited. I do not intend this as an insult."[5]

The movie is based on a book that is written at an elementary school level and is only fifty-eight pages. When I saw the movie on TV, I didn't know it was a book. In the film, William and Sarah discuss her moving to Kansas, and he says,

"Sarah, you don't have to go," William said.
"You're wrong, Will, I do."
"There is plenty of room in the house. Meg wants you to live with us. Nothing has to change."
"Things do change, if you let them."
"You belong here," Will said.
"If I don't go now, I'll never know what it is like to have

---

[5] Patricia MacLachlan, *Sarah, Plain and Tall* (New York: HarperCollins, 1985), 9.

my own life. This is my chance, Will."[6]

Maybe this sounds sappy as you read it and you wonder how on earth God could use such cheesy storytelling for His good. (At least that was my take.) However, I understood Sarah. Like her, I was not mild mannered. Like her, I had a decently comfortable life. I was living in Lawrence, Kansas (oh the irony, as she was moving to Kansas!), and teaching. I had my dream job as I taught both English to international students at the university and math to American middle school students at the local junior high. I remember telling myself to soak it up because it was unlikely I would ever have such an ideal a work situation. Unlike Sarah who had William telling her to stay, several of my colleagues at South Junior High knew that I had also been offered a job to teach in Hawaii. Almost to a person, my coworkers encouraged me to take it, saying, "Kansas will always be here. Go to Hawaii. Go while you are young. Go."

But I had my eye on China. I assured them I would go, just not to Hawaii. As I rewatched the movie in preparation to write this section, I was stumped. I remembered Sarah saying that she wanted her life to count for something. She wanted to invest in something bigger than herself and was responding to the pull to devote herself to something more. Her more was Kansas. My more was God via China. When I moved to China—and when I kept staying—my Chinese

---

6 Yayu Bakamta, "Sarah, Plain and Tall," *Youtube video*, 1:38:45, September 17, 2017. https://www.youtube.com/watch?v=beG9qpRCehw.

students asked me why I lived in China. I referred to this movie again and again. I said that as a Christian I believed I could have served God anywhere in the world. Yet he had gifted me to be a teacher, and China needed native English speakers to be teachers. I loved them, and I wanted to live in such a way that at the end of my life I could look back without regrets.

If you had asked twenty-something Amy what kept her focused the years between the call and the commission, it was the anticipation of a life defined by meaning. Twenty-something Amy knew she had choices, and by obeying God she would be living a more meaningful life. As I look back on pre-field Amy, I appreciate that she was drawn to Sarah, not some oft-referenced cross-cultural worker. Her model lived on a remote farm and invested in three people. Sarah did not change the world, but she did change their world.

My life has been nothing like a Hallmark movie and my taste has moved away from Hallmark. But I own my story. God used that movie to anchor me to His story. Back when I wrote my very first guest post for a blog, guess which movie I referenced when talking about feeling the tug toward wanting a meaningful life? Yup, my girl Sarah, plain and tall.

I wish we were sitting around swapping stories instead of meeting on these pages. You, too, have a story as to what brought you to the field and what kept you focused while you waited. I would love to hear how God pointed you to yourself and beyond yourself to His work in the world. I would love to hear how God takes the universal and makes it particular in your life.

I cannot move on quite yet from the jolt of yesterday. As

I rewatched the scene with Sarah and her brother, William, before she moved, I worked to transcribe it for this section of the book. I played the scene and started typing, then backed up when I got lost. As I played, typed, relistened, and replayed this scene multiple times, a thought began to bubble up. By the third go-through I thought, *Really? The reason Sarah gave William for moving to Kansas was to have her own life? Not that she wanted her life to matter?* That certainly hasn't been the version I've shared the last, oh, nearly thirty years! I'm a bit flummoxed that what I remember God so clearly using isn't a part of the narrative. But it is a part of the narrative I needed, and I am grateful to God that for years I heard what He wanted me to hear. Years later when you revisit your story, who knows, it might contain a message in it that wasn't there, but God used it all the same.

~~~

All the -Ing in the World
A pattern began to emerge as I analyzed the answers to the next survey question, "Before you went to the field, what did you anticipate with excitement about your life on the field?" As I did with every question, I printed off the responses and read through them, taking notes in a notebook. However, with this question about halfway through the first page I noticed something interesting and started a list in the upper right corner on the first page of responses:

Being
Sharing

Working
Teaching
Doing
Living
Studying
Getting to
Seeing
Following
Learning

    I'm sure you notice the pattern too. When asked what the survey participants anticipated, most people answered with an -ing word. I continued adding to the list watching it grow down the right side of the page.

Starting
Serving
Exploring
Building
Supporting
Accomplishing
Experiencing
Meeting
Contributing
Returning
Training
Impacting
Obeying
Exposing ("myself and my children to a new culture")

GETTING STARTED

   I was at the bottom of the page, but not at the end of the answers. I wrote the next wave of responses along the bottom of the page from right to left, following the perimeter of the page clockwise.

Planting
Making a difference
Preaching
Leading
Telling
Loving
Anticipating

   By this point I was practically cheering on each new -ing word and kept listing them from the bottom, now up the left side of the page.

Opening
Fulfilling
Establishing
Interacting
Persevering
Relying
Fellowshipping
Partnering
Saving
Adapting
Discipling
Leaving
Traveling

Growing
Investing

And then I came to the top of the page and wrote three final words along the top.

Dedicating
Improving
Bringing

Look at that list. Quite a thing of beauty, isn't it? When such an obvious pattern emerged, I sensed God smile and tilt his head, saying to us, "That, my dear children, is the language of anticipation. It is the language of hope. It is part of your native heart language."

Now, I know some of you reading are wicked smart when it comes to grammar or survey construction and might be thinking that people answered in -ing words because of how I asked the question. While it is true that the question "Before you went to the field, what did you anticipate with excitement about your life on the field?" is prone to an -ing answer, not everyone used one. For instance, one person answered, "I was excited to make new friends and love people deeply, as I learned their culture." Another wrote, "New experiences and people, a sense of purpose and service." Grammar is part of the -ing pattern to be sure, but something else is going on.

Excitement taps into a different part of you than anticipating challenges. True, you need to be wise about dangers and difficulties you may face, but it's also helpful to think about the positive experiences you're looking forward to. Take a moment to notice where in your body you carry excitement.

Grammar and You

I had a vague recollection of -ing grammar, but I needed Google to remind me that not all -ing words are the same: they could be gerunds, verbal nouns, or present participles[7]. I went down a rabbit trail trying to figure out the difference between gerunds, a state verb, and an action verb.[8] In truth, though a gerund is a verb "which is used as if it were a noun,"[9] a state verb expresses an action that is "relatively static,"[10] and active verbs "express activities, processes, momentary actions, or physical conditions."[11] With these definitions in mind I went back to the list. Most of the -ing words used were gerunds or state verbs. In other words, people did not answer so often with actions they were looking forward to doing; rather it was *who they would be* through the actions they would be doing. Here are some examples:

"Being a servant for the Lord, supporting my husband in his dream, living in a different environment."

"Working in a project that had long been planned for and

---

7 "Gerunds and -ing words in English," Linguapress English Grammar, https://linguapress.com/grammar/gerunds.htm.
8 "State Verbs and Action Verbs," Grammaring, https://www.grammaring.com/state-verbs-and-action-verbs.
9 Gerunds," Linguapress English Grammar.
10 State Verbs," Grammaring.
11 Ibid.

anticipated. Building local friendships. Being able to communicate (I'd visited before when I had no language and went back after language school)."

"Making a difference in the lives of disadvantaged kids—showing them God's love in tangible ways."

"Working with the children, living in Africa."

"I must admit I actually wasn't that excited about going overseas as this was not my first experience of cross-cultural work and I knew how challenging it was likely to be! However, I was anticipating having an opportunity to serve the local people and to get involved in a cause that I believed God had laid close to my heart and was calling me into."

What did many cross-cultural workers anticipate with excitement? Who they would be on the field. This question pointed to a deeply personal place: identity. And it was an identity that exuded hope and promise and positivity.

Will everything you anticipate come to be? Not likely in the first year, but over time I encourage you to revisit what you imagined before you went to the field and watch for the unexpected ways God fulfills the longings He placed in you. As Dr. Martin Luther King Jr. said, "Faith is taking the first step even when you don't see the whole staircase." If faith is the first step, hope is who you will be as you ascend the staircase.

This year, protect and treasure whom you are becoming. Protect and treasure the meaning that your life is taking on. Protect and treasure the fact that while you may not change the entire world, you will change the world of a few who are known and loved by their Heavenly Father.

2
Somewhere Between Awful and Amazing

Teach In China (TIC) arranged for the first-year people to fly as a group, all ninety or so of us. To this day, I shudder at the phrase "group flight" because traveling internationally in a herd is a slice of hell on earth. The lines, the luggage trucks, the eternal checking of passports and visas, and jockeying for who was sitting near the bathroom or baby or whatever. Awful.

En masse we landed in Beijing late at night and were greeted at the airport by another herd of school officials representing the forty or so schools we would scatter to after a few days of touring, getting over jet lag, and beginning to adjust to this new culture. Even though it was late at night, Xiao Luo (Miss Luo), the school official from our school, took Erin, my teammate, and me to dinner at our hotel. Jet lag exhaustion combined with plastic chopsticks equaled a stressful opportunity to make a good first impression, but we powered through. A Chinese phrase I learned much later would have been so helpful: *"Ai ya!"* ("Oh my!")

In my journal, after the second day of touring—also en masse around Beijing—I wrote, "Went to bed last night at 9:15 so was awake before 6:00 a.m. this morning. I decided that our theme song could be a line from a Green Day song that asks if the listener has time to listen to the singer whine about something and nothing at the same time. That seems to sum up my feelings from yesterday. Doing life in a crowd is getting old, but today has been emotionally much better than the last days in California! Breakfast was very Chinese this morning and I don't know if I will ever adjust to seaweed in the morning."

Survey Says

At some point during your first year, you will find yourself whining about everything and nothing at the same time. Even though I filled three journals my first year on the field, this book isn't about me; it's about your first year and all that you will experience. As I mentioned in the previous chapter, I created a ten-question survey and shared it through websites that work with the cross-cultural population. Here are the ten questions:

1. On a scale of 1 (awful) to 10 (amazing), what number would you give your first year?
2. Why did you give the number you gave?
3. Before you went to the field, what did you anticipate being hard or challenging parts of your first year?
4. What ended up being three of the hardest or challenging parts of your first year?
5. Before you went to the field, what did you anticipate with excitement about your life on the field?
6. As you look back on your first year, share three of the highlights from that year.

7. What did you learn about yourself during your first year?
8. What did you learn about God during your first year?
9. What would you like to tell your first-year self?
10. Contact information. [This was the only optional question. I wanted people to be able to participate anonymously so they could say whatever they wanted.]

I launched the survey and answers flooded in! As you can tell from the questions, the focus of the survey wasn't on demographical information such as any specific organization, location, or type of work; instead, I wanted to hear stories. In pouring over the 184 answers, some demographic information appeared. Both men and women answered, most were with specific organizations, and a few participants were on the field independently. The work people were involved in varied, including language teaching, offering medical services, planting fellowships (this book uses language that is accessible around the world), translating the Good Book, and serving marginalized people. Often the first year on the field was dedicated to language study. In addition, the survey represented people living and serving in all nooks and crannies of the world. Some survey participants have been on the field for decades, others a few years, and a few still in their first year. One was fifteen. Of the 184 people who participated, only seven did not include contact information, which means that I was able to ask follow-up questions if needed.

If I had taken the survey, I would have given my first year a nine. Honestly, I would have given it a ten, but I was colder that winter than I had ever imagined a person could be above freezing (more about that later when we talk about the weather), and then there were the mice. I was told the first night, "Mind your doors, Chengdu is famous for mice." Infamous is more like it! Despite minding the doors, the mice still found a way in. So rodents and not being able to feel my feet for several months knocked my ten to a nine.

During my own first year I thought everyone had a fairly—if not outright—positive first-year experience, but I sensed I was on the high end of happy. I downplayed how delighted and content I was so as not to flaunt my happiness. Given my leaning toward one end of the spectrum, the responses to the question both surprised and didn't surprise me. I was surprised how evenly distributed the numbers were, but I was not surprised that every single number was represented. While the responses did not form a perfect bell shape, they were not far off. Here is the breakdown in percentages:

22 percent rated their first year 1–3
23 percent rated their first year 4 or 5
48 percent rated their first year 6–8
7 percent rated their first year 9 or 10

In other words, almost a quarter said it was awful, another quarter said it was bad to average, nearly a half said it was good, and a small slice said it was amazing. Let's spend a bit more time reflecting on the numbers before we dive into why people gave the numbers they did. Roughly 45 percent rated their first year between a one and a five. Said in another way, one out of every two people did not have an amazing first year. Sit with this for a moment. It is easy to think that because God called you, the Red Sea is going to part and you will cross to the field on dry land, so to speak. That was not the case for half of your fellow cross-cultural workers; their transition was less like the Red Sea parting and more like the ten plagues. On the other hand, 55 percent rated their year between a six and a ten, making it roughly half who had a pretty good to great first year.

These stats are a little too close to a game we used to play as children when trying to figure out the future using a flower. Alternating between two options, we would pluck a petal saying, "He loves me," pluck. Then, "He loves me not," pluck. "The first year is going to be awful," pluck. "The first year is going to be amazing," pluck. As I neared the end of the petals, I remembering counting ahead and figuring out which option would be the final answer. I wish I could tell you that if you read this book, pluck, you have increased your chances to move toward amazing, pluck. While the goal of this book is certainly to help you in your first year, it is by no means a miracle cure-all. Nothing is. We all have to live through what our first year brings us, whether it's a ten or a one. But I promise that God will be right there with you every step of the way.

Another element that came through in the survey answers was the sense of a scale, a weighing of two opposites—I could picture the handheld scales used in street markets. Over and over I read a version of either "While parts of that year were really hard, others were so sweet the good outweighs the bad" or "Yes, it had up moments, but the bad was so awful." Someone who rated their year a seven said, "It was a pretty smooth transition and I made some great friendships that year. But it was also rich, awkward, and challenging."

Numbers can also be subjective. One person said, "I have a gift of minimizing the negative memories and enshrining the positive!" I can relate. In truth, when I look back, I tend to emphasize either the good or the bad. The idea of a scale that weighs this *and* that, rather than either/or, will be helpful for you as you live your first year in your new location. This type of scale creates the space for you to experience both the awful and the amazing.

People's explanations of their year held the real treasures to this question. I found myself wanting to interrupt people in my mind with my own commentary on *their* experience. Commenting is easier than actually listening. So, instead of telling you what I thought or injecting my commentary into every section, let's listen to people directly. If you are like me, dying to respond or interject your own experience, join me in practicing listening.

Cultural Influences

"So many logistical puzzles and so little local knowledge to solve them. Family stress, language puzzles, bureaucratic encounters compounded the misery."

"Along with language learning and trying to learn how to feed our family, I was navigating an uprising, influenced by incredible poverty, and an increasingly violent element."

"I loved my host country right away. The people are wonderful, helpful, and amazing. My team dropped the number down."

"It was cold, war-torn, and we couldn't find housing. The team situation was so very difficult and I was a new mom."

"It was amazing and memorable for our family. Language school and learning to homeschool were both things that grounded me in some sense of routine. What keeps it from being amazing is that I didn't know how to relate to other expats and my leaders were not relationally gifted in loving and supporting people through enculturation."

"We (my family and I) had a super-easy transition. Our new home was home within a couple weeks. We were welcomed into a lovely community and had very little culture shock. The only negatives were a political coup within one month of arrival—it was not dangerous, but disruptive—and the lack of infrastructure made communication with those we left behind very challenging."

The Work Itself

"It was magical, exceeded expectations, I accomplished the goals and the year taught me so much, which was useful and inspirational down the road."

"I loved my job, teaching MK's in second and third grade. I taught in a wonderful little school with great kids and staff. It was idyllic in many ways. I knew I was right where God wanted me to be. What keeps this from being a ten is that I was on loan from one organization to another. I fit in perfectly with the group I was on loan to, but not with my sending organization team. Attempts to alleviate the tension and work out the issues were met with resistance and denial by leadership. We finally just worked at loving on the families in our team—even the ornery non-friendly ones. Love wins the day!!"

"My first year was extremely challenging, especially the first six months. I struggled with a lack of identity as the role I had believed I was going to fill did not eventuate. I therefore missed my home country and the job that I left behind and struggled with doubts about whether I was supposed to be there or not. I also had a couple organizational conflicts to navigate, challenging me to really draw into God, seek the support of my friends and family, and hold onto my own sense of integrity. I also had to learn to forgive and move on."

Team/Community Influences

"I entered into a great community (both local and expat) who really helped me get my feet on the ground in my new location. With their support I was able to transition and figure out all the stressful things without too much trouble, and learned a lot about myself and God. I made some wonderful friends that year whom I still keep in contact with, and had so many great experiences."

"We were blessed to meet so many new people who kept us on keel, and helped us whenever we didn't understand and could not find what we thought we needed, and shored us up when we needed it. We did the same for other newbies."

"I had a team leader with some serious emotional issues. We had some serious conflicts and no local support. I was lonely and constantly berated. I struggled with learning how to teach and had no support there either. In addition to all this, when someone sympathetic came along, that blessing soon turned into a sinful situation where I was way too attached to him. It was the loneliest and darkest year of my life."

Organizational Influences

"I was incredibly lonely and my organization did very little to help me adjust. The first year was really a mix between loving where I was and what I was doing and hating it and thinking I was crazy for doing it."

"Our project fell apart, we were robbed by the local pastor we were working for, and we had to change organizations and cities."

"We came into a team that was quick to embrace us and put us right to work—which was both good and bad. There was a lot of activity and (seemingly) fruit, which was encouraging. As we were seconded due to visa issues, there was also a lot of confusion as to roles and leadership."

Personal Influences

"It would have been a higher number, but the first year was tough on our kids, and so it was tough on us."

"I had an excellent time, but also my mom got cancer and had major surgery and my aunt and grandpa died."

"Where to begin. Around a month or two before leaving for the field, I learned that my husband was addicted to pornography. This was a revelation that I would not have guessed in a million years. For reasons that are obvious, as well as other reasons too lengthy to go into here, I was devastated. I questioned whether we were even supposed to be going on the field with THIS. In the end (again, shortening the story), I felt clear direction to continue this journey, so we did. Looking back, moving to China at this time seems ridiculous, so I have to hold tight to, again, what I feel was an absolute 'Go.' I score the year a 'six' versus, say, a two because I absolutely loved my new job and students."

"I had too many transitions: having my first child, death of a loved one, and limited finances."

"Living the Dream" Influences

"It was HARD! But halfway through it, I was suddenly 'home' and it became amazing."

"It was so different but even better than I expected. Challenging but rewarding."

"We had cross-cultural work on our hearts and this was IT! Good African friends and cross-cultural workers around us. Comfortable living for my family. Ministry was what we were hoping for."

"I was just so excited to be there! My arrival felt like it was the fulfillment of the biggest promise I'd been waiting to receive so far in my young life. And it seemed like every day I was hearing the voice of God so clearly as He taught me how to love people."

"It took twelve years of dreaming, disappointments, and planning to get here. We had so many big ideas. We are independent, no organization, but had a network of family, friends, and churches behind us. That meant no guidelines or regular intervals of debriefing or help for daily needs. Still . . . our passion didn't waiver much that first year."

~~~

To Those Not in Their First Year
While this book is intended for those of you in your first year on the field, I realize not all of you are. Maybe you are a parent and want to understand what your child may experience; or you are a member care person from your organization; or you are the teammate who is in his seventh year and has lost that "first-year feeling." You can be instrumental in influencing

first-year family members or teammates who are not having an amazing year.

The following survey response reads like a case study and highlights the crucial role you can play. The participant referenced how her senior cross-cultural workers downplayed her experiences that first year. It got me thinking about how easily I could have been one of the people who downplayed what she was saying if we were teammates and it was years into my time on the field.

> In the first three months, my one-year-old daughter got malaria four times, and she also had typhoid, croup, and an unexplained bright red rash from head to toe. All while we were trying to learn a new language and how to live in Africa. (What?! You have to bleach vegetables?!) Then we moved to where we were supposed to be stationed, in yet another country. There we had to learn another new language. Shortly after we arrived, the government was overthrown by rebels and we were living in a state of unrest as we worried that the rebels would make their way to our small village. I wanted to leave, but the senior cross-cultural workers "had been through this before and weren't worried." I felt trapped and unheard. Then suddenly the rebels did make it to our village and we had to evacuate. I remember putting my daughter's car seat in the car and trying to decide where would be the safest place for it so that she would not be hit by a bullet. We then had to travel six hours on a road meant for a motorcycle and ferry our car on a hand-pulled raft across the river to get to a safe

country. After we evacuated, we then stayed in a different place for a couple months hoping we could return to our house. I was depressed, scared, and living in limbo. We eventually went back to the States for a few months before returning to a different town in the same country. All through my first year I kept on saying, "Why does this have to be so hard?!"

Wow, let's briefly tally up all this family had going on: language study, learning how to do life, repeated illness early on—not only repeated, but four different kinds of serious illnesses, moving to a different country, political unrest that escalated, then another move. By any account, this is an extremely challenging first year. The phrase *I felt trapped and unheard* jumped out at me when I first read this. No one wants to feel trapped and unheard. Ever. But during your first year on the field, when so much is new and support systems are still being built, *trapped and unheard* is isolation on steroids.

(Briefly back to first-year people reading this section: if "trapped and unheard" is the phrase that describes what you are experiencing, I encourage you to risk reaching out. You know your situation better than I do, but you may want to reach out to family, friends, or a church back home, teammates, leadership in your organization, online websites geared toward cross-cultural workers, or even a counselor who works with cross-cultural workers from a distance. These are just a few options. There are resources available, sometimes even more than we think. Talk to someone you trust. They can help you sort out whether or not what you are experiencing is reasonable, suggest others you might need to talk to, be an outside ear to bounce ideas off of, and pray for you.)

How can you, the family member or teammate, help your first-year person and maybe help a "five" year become a "seven"? Universally vital is your ability to be empathetic. Empathy fuels connection between you and your loved one or teammate. Jade Panugan quoting Brené Brown said, "Empathy is a choice, in order to connect with you, I have to connect with that feeling in me."[12] You may not have been in the same situation as your friend, daughter, or nephew; it doesn't matter. Brené Brown adds that "empathy is not connecting to an experience, it's connecting to the emotions that underpin an experience. If you've ever felt grief, disappointment, shame, fear, loneliness, or anger, you're qualified."[13]

Hearing your loved one's struggles might release your inner warrior. If you feel yourself trying to make it better, stop, take a breath and listen. Most of us have the superpower of rescuing, helping, or trying to solve problems; whatever you call it, the irony is that this superpower is not as much about your loved one or teammate as it is about you. I hate when I cannot help a friend. I hate when I feel powerless. I hate when I do not have access to resources that could solve a problem. I hate these feelings so much, I will jump into action so I do not have to feel the pain and discomfort. I bet

---

[12] Jade Panugan, "Brené Brown on Empathy & Sympathy," Craftdeology, http://www.craftdeology.com/brene-brown-empathy-sympathy/.
[13] Brené Brown, *Dare to Lead: Brave Work, Tough Conversations, Whole Hearts* (New York: Random House, 2018), 140.

some of you are the same. Each one of us can grow in our ability to sit with people in difficult situations.

Job's friends show how challenging it can be to stay in "listen" mode without jumping to "solving" mode. When they heard of the great tragedy that Job had experienced, "they set out from their homes and met together by agreement to go and sympathize with him and comfort him" (Job 2:11). I'm right there with Job's friends. I am probably a little too proud that my Crisis Counseling professor dubbed me "good with a crisis."

The story continues, "When they saw him from a distance, they could hardly recognize [Job]; they began to weep aloud, and they tore their robes and sprinkled dust on their heads. Then they sat on the ground with him for seven days and seven nights. No one said a word to him, because they saw how great his suffering was" (Job 2:12–13). So far, so good.

In my recollection of this passage, Job's friends jumped in with suggestions and began to depart from the empathy script, so to speak. But my recollection was wrong and had me skipping ahead in the story. After hearing of Job's situation and sitting with him, Eliphaz the Temanite, Bildad the Shuhite, and Zophar the Naamathite still did not speak; instead, it is Job who spoke first. "After this, Job opened his mouth and cursed the day of his birth" (Job 3:1). Job expounded on his misery for the next twenty-six verses. He ended with, "What I feared has come upon me; what I dreaded has happened to me. I have no peace, no quietness; I have no rest, but only turmoil" (Job 3:25–26).

When I put myself sitting with Eliphaz, Bildad, and Zophar, I remind myself that seven days have passed. Sure,

Job is still in shock. Sure, his loss has been great. But I find myself thinking, *Really? This is what you feared would happen? You feared you would lose everything?* And out the window goes my empathy. I understand why Eliphaz replied, "If someone ventures a word with you, will you be impatient?" (Job 4:2). Look how thoughtfully he brought up his own opinion. *Can I venture a word with you?* Here is the nugget you and I need to cling to when it comes to empathy: "Rarely does a response make something better. Connection is what makes things better."[14]

Two months after moving to Chengdu, my teammate Erin and I took a ten-hour bus ride to visit the closest team from our organization. We had gone through our training with Cynthia and the Brunkmans, and we were looking forward to seeing some familiar faces. The bus ride to Nanchong was stressful because our language ability was almost nonexistent. As the ride went on and on, I tried to ask those around me if we were indeed on the road to Nanchong. Using my phrase book, they found the phrase, "There isn't." To this day I can remember the feeling in my stomach as we rode on that bus. *There isn't.* We were on the wrong bus. "At worst," I said to Erin as we considered our options, "we can just get off the bus, cross the street, and get on another bus heading back to Chengdu." It was a plan, but that did not ease the ache of helplessness in my stomach.

---

14 Brené Brown as quoted by Hannah Rose, "How to Show Up For Grief," *Psychology Today*, July 15, 2019, https://www.psychology-today.com/za/blog/working-through-shame/201907/how-show-grief?amp.

Afterward, if a family member or member care person had said, "Can I venture a word with you?" after I told the story and then proceeded to say, "What were you thinking?" or "Why didn't you check before you got on the bus?" or "At least you had each other . . . when I first traveled I was all by myself or with all of my screaming children or whatever makes my situation so much worse than yours"—any one of those responses might have resulted in me punching the speaker in the face (at least in my mind), the opposite of making me feel better about my bus ride situation. Instead of a good response, what I needed was a connection. If you have ever felt helpless and out of control and sacred, and you tapped into that feeling with a response as simple as "How scary!" or "Wow, you'll never forget that trip!" I would feel connected to you. And as Brené Brown said, "Connection is what makes it better."

Turns out, *there isn't* was the closest phrase my bus friend could find in my phrase book. What he meant was "We aren't there yet." It was not until midnight, when we finally stepped off the bus, hunting for a taxi, and saw Cynthia and Patty waving in a sea of Chinese, that we knew for sure *there is*!

Been There, Done That

A few words for the senior cross-cultural worker who has been through the experience of having new teammates, I get it. I do. You have your own first-year experience. And if you are in your fifth, eighth, or twenty-seventh year, first-year people tend to comment about the same things and you might be tired of hearing same old same old. I know I grew tired of them. Some days my patience well ran deep and I could listen with genuine interest and empathy to rough cultural experiences or share in their excitement over a positive encounter. However, to my regret, other days my patience well ran bone dry. On the surface I was listening, but I'm sure it was evident I wasn't really listening.

When this happens, it's easy for me to think that it's the other person who is draining; but if I'm honest, when it comes to the difference between deep well versus dry well, this comes from within. Maybe I had not gotten enough sleep, or was in the midst of a very stressful week and felt overwhelmed, or simply wanted to be doing something else that I thought was more important (or interesting) than listening to my first-year friend.

In these moments, remind yourself that you need your first-year colleague. You need their fresh eyes. You offer experience to your teammate; they offer freshness to you. See them as a resource. Ask questions to help you see the situation through their eyes. And remember to practice empathy, to look for the common feelings, not the common experiences. Even though you live and serve in the same country, if you only look for shared experiences, you miss the opportunity to connect and help their first year be more amazing and less awful.

Friends, Family, and Empathy

I remember when it hit me, about two days after arriving in Beijing, that the longest I had known anyone in my new daily life was a month. One whole month. In truth, that month of training and transitioning to the field was intensely bonding, but still it could not replace people and relationships that were years in the making and predated my China life.

Your history with your friend or family member is the gift you have to offer them. They want to share their lives with you. They want to tell you about the exciting new experiences, the confusing experiences, and the very annoying and frustrating experiences they are having. But they will filter what they share with you based on your reactions.

Try to be aware when you are in awe of them (also called the *pedestal effect*). Yes, your son is brave for moving to the other side of the world. Yes, your daughter is to be lauded for responding to the call of God. But they are also still normal human beings. Normal human beings who might live in rather exotic, remote, or unusual places. What you, as their pre-field person, are being asked to do is to lean into the tension of the exciting and overwhelming first year with them. Be aware of your own personality. Are you one who loves excitement and tends to downplay the less pleasant emotions? Then be sure you are also being empathetic to the overwhelming. Are you the kind of person who doesn't want to get carried away with how fun and exciting their new life is so you pay more attention to the hard parts? Your challenge will be to make space to enjoy and celebrate all of the—hopefully—fun firsts with your friend or family member.

Daniel Pink says, "Empathy is about standing in someone else's shoes, feeling with his or her heart, seeing with his or her eyes . . . Not only is empathy hard to outsource and automate, but it makes the world a better place."[15] I would add, empathy makes the world a better place, because your

---

15 Daniel Pink, *A Whole New Mind: Why Right-Brainers Will Rule the Future* (New York: Penguin Group, 2005), 159; 171.

ability to express empathy with your child or friend in their first year on the field will directly impact them. And who knows, you just may move them from having a "three" year to having a "six" year. While teammates and local friends can empathize, those who have known the individual prior to the field and the longest play a unique role in providing empathy during this first year.

~~~

Back to First-Year Folks
While it is possible your first year will either be awful or amazing, most likely your first year will be somewhere in between. It might be like this:

> "My first year was amazing! Everything was new and exciting, from the food to the culture around me. I joined a loving, supportive team. I had the opportunity to learn a new language full-time. I made new friends. My first year was also hard. Everything was new and scary, from the food to the culture around me. I joined a team, whom I had to now live with, filled with broken humans just like me. I struggled with not being able to speak the language around me well for most of that first year. I grieved not having my friends and precious family in the same country. That first year was emotionally draining. Everything I knew and had learned about cross-cultural work was tested."

What might your first year hold? The new and exciting.

Maybe a supportive team. What you know may be tested. You may have periods of profound loneliness and grief. You may see God work in life-changing ways. Possibly all or some of the above simultaneously. As your year moves along, my hope, especially if your year is challenging, is that you see yourself reflected in the pages of this book and experience the sense that you are not alone.

3
Welcome to You

Serving Jesus cross-culturally sounded noble. And well, it is noble. But somehow I translated noble into "because you are following a noble and important call, you will turn into the best version of yourself." If only. My journal from that first year is scattered with a fairly steady stream of the times I became annoyed or frustrated. For example, take this "noble" entry written two months into my time on the field:

> After grading the students' papers, I went to the dorms to return the papers and invite two of the girls over for a pancake dinner. I was in Zhu Hui's room chatting with the boys when word came that Erin was looking for me. The dean of the English Department had come over to let us know we would be having dinner with visitors from the countryside school we would visit. We have been invited to teach at their school one weekend in December and Dean Yu said yes. Ugh. We are ticked because it means no pancakes and postponing library hours with the students. Erin and I played Rook while we waited for dinner. (Of course they were late, but I think it was the train's fault.) Six people from their school took us out to dinner and none spoke to us. What kills

me is that the only reason they came was to take us out to dinner and then go home the next day! We ate at a hot pot restaurant and actually only the president of their school sat with us while the others sat at another table. The food was quite good, but my intestines felt a bit weird. After dinner Erin walked over to the library and I walked home with Dean Yu. I grabbed the papers I needed to return to students and headed over to the library to join Erin. Thus goes another day in Chengdu.

Please do not mishear me. It is expected and okay to have negative reactions to situations that are annoying, disturbing, unjust, or unfair. However, what sadly comes through loud and clear in my journals is how wronged I felt when an injustice—according to my American-culture definition of the word—occurred against me. In this instance, I was ticked when I had to change plans last minute *and* could not have pancakes (a double injustice, in my first-year opinion). Oh, Amy. In fairness, I would have said that it was not so much about the pancakes as about the assumption that we would drop our plans and be honored to go out to dinner. To my sense of manners, it would have been thoughtful to ask if we had plans or if we would be willing to change them.

Many years later, I understand culturally why this wouldn't happen in China, but in your first year you do not know the culture as well as you will come to know it. What you can know is your reaction to your experience. In your first year, you will see yourself from an angle that only your first year on the field can offer. This year is a unique gift from God to you. Through the often purifying fire of this once-in-a-lifetime year, parts of yourself you possibly weren't aware of will be exposed. Thank the merciful Lord that sometimes your reaction will surprise you and you will glimpse parts of yourself that make you proud.

What I see as I have reread my journals for this book is that I am usually up for an adventure and have a very low need for information to feel comfortable. I also see that I define adventure as anything that sounds fun. So a taxi ride could be an adventure, a conversation with a student could be an adventure, a weekend teaching at an extremely poor countryside school could be an adventure. Before moving to the field, I enjoyed life. What my first year helped me see is that one of the best parts of the true me is that I see potential wonder and fun around almost every corner. Not knowing the language (so often I had no clue what was going on around me) and not knowing anyone I was now living with prior to that year revealed this part of myself more clearly. Some of what you learn this year will be evident right away, as you live it. Other aspects will unfold over time.

You Are That Person

Even though you have been called by God for the noble task of bringing the Good News to places that need it, God does not view you as a stepping stone in this great cause. In His grand scheme, He is at least as interested, perhaps even more so, in working *in* you as *through* you. We are camping on this point a bit because so many come to the field chomping at the bit, ready to serve. It is understandable—after all that you went through to get here, all you gave up to be here, all you have invested—that you are eager. But maybe this year will

GETTING STARTED

hold moments like the one in 2 Samuel when Nathan told David a story about a poor man. The New Living Translation describes the man this way: "The poor man owned nothing but one little lamb he had bought. He raised that little lamb, and it grew up with his children. It ate from the man's own plate and drank from his cup. He cuddled it in his arms like a baby daughter. One day a guest arrived at the home of the rich man. But instead of killing an animal from his own flock or herd, he took the poor man's lamb and killed it and prepared it for his guest" (2 Samuel 12:3–4). No surprise, David was furious, declaring that any man who did this deserved to die. But Nathan simply responded, "You are that man" (2 Samuel 12:7 NLT), revealing parts of David to himself.

Or take Peter who boldly told Jesus he would never disown him, yet within a few hours Peter had denied Jesus not once but three times, just as Jesus had foretold. Luke writes that after the third denial the rooster crowed and Jesus "turned and looked straight at Peter." Peter "went outside and wept bitterly" (Luke 22:60–62). After His resurrection, Jesus showed Peter that even when he failed Jesus, it was not the end of the story. Peter was still qualified to "feed my sheep" (John 21:15–17).

"This is the very beginning of a long journey that will shape you if you let it." One survey participant said when she answered what she would tell her first-year self, "Embrace it and seek out what you can learn about God, yourself, and others from the hard times. Do not let people walk over you, but listen and be teachable." She went on to tell her first-year self, "Hold your theology with open hands and let God shape it. Approach every thought and conversation (even the ones with people from your passport country) with the thought that the worldview that you grew up with is but only one in the world . . . and God loves, embraces, and challenges all worldviews."

You might find it a relief to be far away from dysfunctional families or situations. Even so, your new environment will be different enough that how you coped with stress—regardless of how healthy or unhealthy your home was—might not work on the field. In the process of adjusting, the good, the bad, and the ugly of you will bubble up to the surface. The good might be a welcome surprise, the bad, a source of personal disappointment, and the ugly, a place for open-heart surgery. Thankfully, God in His mercy is in the business of transformation for your good and His glory.

One last interesting note about self-discovery: the survey participants consistently answered a question I did not ask, so I figured I needed to pay attention. In the unique liminal space of the first year with the old life gone and the new life being built, participants kept telling me what they learned about themselves, even though I never asked. I thought this was curious and took a closer look at their answers and why they might be sharing these details despite not being asked. When I considered their responses, the answers fell into four broad categories: *Relationships and You*, *Personal Characteristics*, *Your Identity*, and *Your Personal Wiring*. The next section of this chapter will look at how God may work in these four areas.

GETTING STARTED

Relationships and You

One of the greatest ways to see yourself afresh during your first year on the field is in how you interact with people. Between teammates, others in your organization serving in different locations, and all of the locals you will meet, the opportunities to interact are endless. You will come to have moments from your first year seared into your memory so that when you look at them with "time binoculars," they will come into crisp detail.

Erin and I spent only three weeks with our fellow trainees before we each went to our assignment. I was not prepared for how much I would cry when it came time to say goodbye to them, in particular my new friend and province mate Cynthia. Using my time binoculars, I see Erin and myself hugging Cynthia on the steps of the Friendship Hotel in Beijing before she left for her school, tears running down my cheeks. Did I say crying? Sobbing would be more like it. Sobbing over someone I had not even known a month. I knew it would be hard when I said goodbye to my family, so I was emotionally prepared, but I had not seen this gut-wrenching goodbye coming. I didn't realize how quickly and deeply attached we had become.

Here are a few of the ways people saw themselves in a different light when it came to relating to others:

"I was a really good language learner. But I also sadly learned that I was not a nice person to those around me when our stress levels were high. I didn't want to accept that my responses were my fault and that I needed to find healthier ways to deal with the high stress."

WELCOME TO YOU

"I came to realize that I was not the organization's savior."

"I had to learn the lesson that I can't try to please everyone, and I can't avoid conflict."

"I am a better communicator in my marriage when all of the crutches and distractions are gone."

"I didn't like the person I became/saw that first year on the field. Plus, I had panic attacks and a team leader/boss who just wanted to fix me."

"I had to face up to how bad I was at handling conflict. (Thankfully, I learned a LOT that year about resolving conflict in a way that makes Jesus happy.)"

"(Sadly) I thought I was better than the local people and even God's gift to them, and this was hugely unhelpful in learning and developing relationships."

When asked, "What would you like to tell your first-year self?" one person said the following:

"I would tell myself to go talk to people! Lower your standard of friendship and invite them to your house for tea after only one short conversation. Prioritize learning the language and use it all the time even though you feel like a little kid. Don't let being an introvert become an excuse—if you are isolated long enough, you'll be dying for company so bad that you might morph into a semi-extrovert anyway. Get ahead of the curve by making friends so that down the road you can have those one-on-one visits you like so much. Don't worry too much about acting like a foreigner. You can't fully assimilate no matter how hard you try, and you'll just wear yourself out. Focus on loving people; they'll recognize it."

Whether with fellow language learners, your spouse, those in your organization, or people in your daily life, you will not lack for opportunities to interact. Even if you don't need to push yourself to interact with people, give yourself breaks; it is okay not to talk to everyone. This is a lesson I had to learn in the bike lanes of Chengdu when stopped at red lights and strangers would ask if I would be their friend and want my telephone number. It's a balancing act. You do need people in your life. You need friends. When what you see in your interactions disappoints you, gently remind yourself God could have used any moment to show you this about yourself and He chose that moment because He loves you. Receive these insights not as failures but as opportunities.

Personal Characteristics

One of the highlights of my childhood was summer camp. At the end of every meal we had a short song fest. Many of the songs were silly camp songs, but the song leaders always worked in a few more substantive songs. To this day, if I want to remember "The Fruit of the Spirit" from Galatians, I will hum, "But the fruit of the Spirit is love, joy, peace, longsuffering, gentleness, goodness, faith, meekness, temperance, against such there is no law. Oh, oh, oh, the fruit of the Spirit is..." as my mind continues on with another round. In full disclosure, since I learned the King James Version and singing about being longsuffering to a catchy, fast-paced tune is not the easiest thing to do, this version of the song has not stood the test of time; I cannot find it online.

What brought back this memory of singing about the fruit of the Spirit was the repetition of the word "patience" used in the survey responses. While many discovered that they were less patient than they hoped, others found that being in a foreign setting actually brought out more patience in them. You might also notice that some of your personal characteristics manifest themselves in ways you have not seen before, either with an abundance or, disappointingly, a lack.

Here are a few of the ways people shared how they saw themselves in a different light when it came to personal characteristics:

"I'm not patient!! Nothing like moving to another country to find that out. I wanted to know the language well in that first year and I wanted to be a part of the rest of the team's ministry straight away."

"I am not as patient as I thought; I am more inclined to sound commanding than I intended!"

"I have more patience in my host country than in my passport country. I enjoy seeing differences in culture and how others do life."

GETTING STARTED

"I learned that I am very proud. I didn't think I was, but boy, my pride took a beating that first year! It was so needed and I am so thankful it happened. I also learned that I have a finite amount of love and patience and that I can't operate out of my own resources. God has to be the one filling me up so I can pour out. I learned I run out really quickly on my own!"

"My patience levels stink! :) I learned how much I need a sabbath every week."

"Stress brought out the worst in me, parts of me that I had never seen before."

"I learned that I have a lot of areas to grow in (humility, trust, confidence). I think the sins that were hiding in my comfortable life in the US were forced to the front of my mind in a new environment and I actually had to deal with them."

"I can be pretty dang prideful. And I am not at all as smart as I thought. I mean I'm smart, but I knew no Chinese, nothing about church planting, nothing about being a good godly roommate . . . so I was pretty dumb and full of myself."

When asked, "What would you like to tell your first-year self?" one person said, "This is going to be way more painful than you can imagine and you are more prideful than you think. Always keep your relationship with God your top priority, your relationship with your family next, and then comes the ministry. You're going to get these priorities mixed up from time to time and it will cause you a lot of pain. Always stay focused on God and your family."

Regardless of what comes up in you, take heart that you will not need to rely solely on camp songs during this first year. I recommend creating a mental picture of God and you for this year based on Zephaniah 3:17: "The LORD your God is with you, the Mighty Warrior who saves. He will take great delight in you; in his love he will no longer rebuke you, but will rejoice over you with singing."

What God shows you about yourself is not meant to shame you. It is to love you as you grow toward your garden-of-Eden, pre-fall self.

Your Identity

While I had a healthy pride in being an American before I moved to China, I would not characterize myself as overly patriotic. I laugh to think how much I came to realize my very Americanness my first year in China. Some of it was silly cultural stuff that makes for good party stories. Why did boarding the bus feel like a full contact sport? Were lines too much to ask for? But other insights about who I am and what is important to me cut deeper. Even though it was years ago, when I recall an oral English class final I administered, I still feel disoriented. I invited groups of six students to my home for an hour-long conversation as their final. One particular group of men told me that people with Down syndrome should not be allowed to be born. They all agreed, casually yet emphatically. I think I pushed back a little, but mostly I thought of my friend Sarah Lynn, a few years my senior, who has Down syndrome. I could not adequately express to

GETTING STARTED

my students how she has enhanced my life. How her family, being friends with my family while Sarah Lynn and I were growing up, had both formalized and normalized the idea that every life matters. Instead of continuing to push the students, after they left I raged to Erin about the cavalier view of life as we prepared dinner.

During this year you will see parts of yourself that are deeply Christian, formed by Scripture and your beliefs. You will also see ways in which your personality, family, life experiences, and home culture have shaped you as a person. Sorting out what you need to keep and what you need to let go of, and how to find a blend, will start this year. As with other areas, some of your identity is beautiful, some will be worth dying to, and parts of it will change based on what you learn in this new land.

Here are a few of the ways people thought about themselves, in a different light when it came to personal identity or the type of person they are:

"I see these three things: I'm not always happy, I can get burnt out easily if I don't practice self-care, and I love sharing Bible stories organically in conversation but sometimes am too eager and don't let my husband share."

"I learned that I didn't know what my boundaries were in this new context. All the normal boundaries I had in the States were something I never thought of. But once I had those boundaries challenged, I realized I had them."

"I have a savior complex. I had pride about having left

materialistic America."

"One thing I learned is that I need a lot of margin and rest times, and need to be intentional about building that into my schedule. Any time I would travel, I would make sure to take an extra day off of language study in order to catch up and rest. I also learned it is okay to need this! The first nine months of living overseas I didn't read a single book, thinking I needed to spend every minute studying language. Yet reading is something that is life-giving to me, and once I allowed myself that 'indulgence,' I actually enjoyed language study more."

"Moving overseas did not change who I am or my limitations."

When asked, "What would you like to tell your first-year self?" identity came up more than *relationships*, *personal characteristics*, or *your personal wiring*. Here are some examples:

"Be yourself. Don't try to be the superhero overseas worker that looks good on paper, or the person mentoring you, or your teammate. You have to be who God created you to be and look for what that looks like in your context. It's okay to need rest, to need help, and to not do things well sometimes. You are not a failure."

"It's okay to be you. Everyone has a different way of doing life and their walk with God. If you feel like a situation is not right at home or at work, it probably isn't. Talk to your roommates if you can. If you can't, find someone to help you debrief what you're going through."

GETTING STARTED

"Don't make yourself have to fit into another cross-cultural worker's mold. Give yourself grace and allow yourself accommodations for your introversion and your age (I landed on the field at fifty-four years old). I realized that a language learning time schedule is only a suggestion, and everyone can't learn at the same rate. Find like-minded people to share life with and don't do hard core if you can't (I was told not to hang with other cross-cultural workers and to make friends with the locals, yet I couldn't talk to them so was alone almost all the time outside of class). Don't go home in the first year if at all possible."

"Your identity is not in your work. Be who you are, just abroad . . . even if your leadership thinks it's slower and less significant than what you SHOULD be doing. The Lord is just as pleased with the two-talent worker as with the five."

Use this year deliberately to find your identity in Christ. Finding your identity in Christ means *believing that what God says about you is truer than what anyone says—including you.* When tempted to believe you are either much better than or much worse than you really are, look to what the Bible says about you instead of what your home or host culture says. In Jesus you do not lose your true self; you become your true self, only in Him.

Your Personal Wiring

Because Erin and I moved to China at the same time, were close in age, and were the only two foreign teachers at our school, we joked we were more married than most married people. We had the same job, boss, and coworkers; we ate all of our meals together; we had daily devotional time together; we socialized together; we worshipped together; we even battled mice and hand-sized spiders together. But after our first ten-hour bus ride to visit friends from training, we learned we would not be traveling on weekends together (other than required trips organized by our school). I found traveling to be one big adventure, and Erin found traveling to be one big stress bomb. She knew herself and wisely said on this first trip, "This is my last trip." Said it in such a way the subject was not up for negotiation and had nothing to do with whether her way was better or worse than my way. The wisdom in knowing herself and her wiring gave us the gift of operating freely with how God had individually made each of us. Here are a few of the ways people saw their wiring in a different light during their first year:

"I am quite flexible and adaptable when situations change."

"I find it very hard to trust God, especially when I can't see any clear evidence of Him working either in me or through me. I learned that God didn't send me onto the field to save the world, He was quite capable of doing that without me!! And that I have a long way to go before I become a good wife, genuinely focused on the well-being of my husband and helping to support him come what may."

"I found out I was able to let go of things I didn't think I could (like privacy) and that I could do things I didn't think I could (like go find people to talk to for the sake of practicing language). And that there is joy in that. The first year is probably the best time in life to embrace humility. So. Much. Opportunity!"

"I have a stronger protector/defender bent than many other people. I have expectations for myself that I would never put on other people. My faith is a lot weaker and I am more vulnerable than I realized."

"I'm strong and selfish and my comforts are important to me. I also saw how much I love new things."

"I learned that I considered myself very adaptable, but I was more 'set in my ways' than I ever wanted to think I was!"

"I have a strong administrative gifting I didn't know existed."

"I am stronger than I think. I will sacrifice pretty much anything to give my family happiness, but that is not always the healthiest thing. I learned to be wiser in my choices."

When asked, "What would you like to tell your first-year self?" one person responded, "You are braver than you think . . . . But at the same time, it's okay to not be brave! It's okay to let those tears fall. Journal. Journal. Journal. Journal the cool things about your new culture, and also the hard things. You won't regret it as it's a great keepsake and it also helps you to process life better."

I wonder what you will come to see about yourself this year. I pray that you will have the courage to own parts of you that are not sinful or wrong, but simply different from your teammates. And be willing to shed the things God brings to light in you that need shedding. Like my teammate Erin and I learned, knowing and accepting how you are made is a unique gift you can give to your team.

Meeting Yourself

As you see yourself in a new light, God knows what you will see. Perhaps what comes out will surprise and delight you; perhaps it might cause you to join Peter in weeping bitterly after that rooster crowed. More likely you will be like this survey participant who captures the paradox of meeting yourself: "I'm not as strong as I thought (yet simultaneously stronger). I need advice and help from people who know better than I do. I am fragile and can break. But at the same time, I *can* do all things through Christ."

Yes, you came to serve others, and I promise, you will. But the lessons you learn this year about yourself will impact your relationships and ministry opportunities long into the future. Use the gift of this first year to learn what God has for you now, knowing that He holds the past, present, and future simultaneously.

4
You Will Be Too (Something)

The walk from my apartment to the classroom I taught in took about ten minutes, seven if I booked it. But if I walked from the classroom back to my apartment with a student? It felt like fifteen hundred years of dragging ourselves through waist-high pudding. Over and over that first year I heard, "You walk so fast." Well, that is what I heard. I believe what they were actually saying is, "You walk too fast." A small road cut through the campus with a gate on each side of the road. Each gate was operated by a guard who had nothing to do but sit in a chair and chat with people who passed by. To be clear, it was not one but two guards I galloped past day after day, giving them opportunity after opportunity to comment to everyone around how fast I walked.

Culturally I was too fast, though I didn't know it at the time. With time I grew to move more slowly and I made peace with what—usually—felt like plodding through invisible pudding.

You might not be too fast of a walker, but you are going to be too something:

Too loud.
Too slow.
Too generous.
Too stingy.
Too single.
Too lazy.
Too hardworking.
(Have) too many children.

 China is a land of ranking. Coming from a culture that espouses equality and the privacy of personal information, it was a shock to my system to hear my teammate and myself compared—out loud—almost as a sport. She was blonde and beautiful; I was not. Turns out, being blonde is the standard of Western beauty in the eyes of the Chinese. I failed before I even started. Because we were a team of two, it was easy to make comparisons. "Erin is beautiful, and, Amy, you are . . . [searching for something kind to say] . . . outgoing!" Hearing this a few times is fine. After all, we did come to a foreign land for a Greater Cause, right? But this refrain was not said a few times; it was said a few hundred times (as luck would have it, often wading through that invisible pudding).

 It became a mantra of "not enough." "You are not as pretty as your teammate." I do not know what Erin heard, but knowing human nature, she probably also heard a message of what she *was not* instead of the truth of who she *was*. This is what "not enough" does—it takes any message spoken and twists it in your mind to be a message of *you are not enough*.

 Can I tell you how long the pause lasted between "Erin is beautiful, and, Amy, you are"—pause, pause,

pause—"outgoing"? Long enough for my mind to fill in the blank—Amy you are loud, large, fat and the list could grow at remarkable speed. I found myself wanting to combat the message of "not enough" with the comfort of a label. *Did you know I was a teacher once selected to help open a new school? Did you know I was the head of a significant committee at church? Did you know that I can read and drive a car on an open highway? Did you know I am a decent singer? Avid sports fan?*

As I planned to go to the field, I loved how I would be identifying with the Son in the incarnational process. If you could have seen inside my head, it was like a Disney set in there. You know that scene where Snow White or Cinderella or any of the female characters almost floats above the ground as she walks, surrounded by happy little animals, carrying a basket of flowers and spreading love, joy, and happiness while singing a lovely song? That was how I pictured myself in China, doing things the Chinese way, carrying the love of Jesus. While I did carry love and joy, the main detail of this scene that I got right was being surrounded by happy little animals. I just hadn't counted on them being mice and battling with them over my precious food mailed from America.

The way you will embody the incarnational process is beautiful. Unfortunately, though, beauty does not equal easy (or come with an award-winning soundtrack). Instead, it comes with far more loss, limitations, and death than my naïve self, accounted for. Paul explains it this way in Philippians 2:6–7: "Who, being in very nature God, did not consider equality with God something to be used to His own advantage; rather, He made himself nothing by taking the very nature of a servant, being made in human likeness."

When you bump into your *too muchness*, use it to point you to Jesus and serving.

Roles You Played

Moving to the field also involves laying aside all or part of the roles you previously played. Pause for a moment and think of six roles you had before you moved to the field. Here are mine: family member (daughter/sister/granddaughter/niece), junior high math teacher, active member of my church, active member of the cross-cultural workers committee at church, roommate, and sports fan. Of course I had other roles, but those were my top six roles. Considering the six roles you've listed, some will die now that you are on the field. For me, the primary role that died was being a public-school teacher in the US. I did not know it at that time, but I wouldn't teach again in US public schools, even though I maintained my license for years after moving. Other roles only died for a season or continued in an altered state.

I am still a daughter, sister, and niece. In the ensuing years, all my grandparents died, and four nieces were born. During my first few years on the field I learned to navigate the changes that come with being a family member on the other side of the world and not physically a part of significant events. This role is where I felt the most deprivation. It is also the role that changed the most, with grandparents dying, parents aging, nieces being born, and other family dynamics. I also felt role deprivation in my paycheck and lack of professional and career advancement, but my heart felt it most deeply in my family roles.

In addition, transitioning to the field makes you aware of

roles that used to be so automatic you may not have noticed them. When I moved to Chengdu, roles I thought were meaningful and added to healthy self-esteem were taken off the table for a while. And parts that I would have defined as "not very meaningful" suddenly took an excessive amount of time. How many of you put "eater" as one of your roles when you made your list? In your passport country, buying and preparing food takes time, but likely nothing like when you go to the field! Keeping myself fed in China took more time than I imagined. Suddenly I was limited by how much I could carry home in one shopping trip (I didn't have a car) and by the size of my (small) refrigerator and (small) toaster oven. Add to that the mental and emotional energy required to figure out how to buy and prep for meals I could actually make. Only to be followed by washing all the dishes by hand (I didn't have a dishwasher) with water I heated on my stove (we only had cold running water).

What you can't tell from my list is the role I felt the guiltiest about. My roommate in Kansas was not merely a roommate; she was my friend. Our morning routine was a well-orchestrated thing of beauty. After exercising at the gym, we took turns showering, eating breakfast, and packing for lunch before heading to work. I dropped Jess at her job on my way to teach and, if it worked out, picked her up after work. I could go on and on about our escapades and adventures in and around Lawrence, Kansas.

The detail I have omitted is this: my friend is legally blind. My leaving meant that she could no longer go to the gym in the mornings because I was not there to drive her, and that she would have to walk to work. Who would go to the movies and sit in the front row with her? Who would be her "seeing eye girl," as I was referred to in public when people were confused about why she needed help? I also doubted I would ever live with anyone as funny as Jess again. My leaving did not mean she simply had to find a new apartment or a new roommate; it led to a drastic change in her life. I understood this was part of the call, and Jesus was worth it, but that did not remove the guilt and sting of this role deprivation and everything it cost my friend as a result.

You too may have a role that others might think is no big deal, but you feel It deeply, like my role with Jess. Here are a couple signs you might be experiencing due to role deprivation:

1. Your emotional responses are out of proportion to a situation. Do you sense yourself under or overreacting to certain scenarios?
2. You notice you are hustling for your worth. Do you sense yourself being defensive or questioning what others think about you or how you use your time?

While role deprivation is unavoidable, naming it helps us make sense of what is going on. Though I did not ask survey participants about being "too something" or role deprivation specifically, several people mentioned it in response to the question, "What ended up being three of the hardest or challenging parts of your first year?" Here are a few examples:

"What ended up being the hardest part of my first year was trying to understand the local culture and, given that

I was a young, single female, feeling as if I had no value or importance."

"Always being the 'vazaha' (white lady) on show whenever I went out in my tiny town, I couldn't go anywhere and just blend into the background. The constant calling out to me and staring—this was very tiring and made me reluctant to leave the relative ease of the hospital compound at times."

"Being seen as a rich 'Mericano all of a sudden when in Australia we'd been on the lower end of the economic scale."

"Figuring out my place in an existing family ministry."

"Just living and existing in my host country. For instance, trying to get groceries without being harassed by gross men or trying to find something to do where my 'whiteness' didn't stand out so much; finding out that even though I had come to do one job on the field, I was needed for another position. I was put in that role and was expected to get our project out of the $20,000 worth of debt that my teammates had incurred."

"Juggling language school with motherhood and pregnancy; in addition to identity as a language learner, not as a classroom teacher."

"Distance from our children especially during significant life events and the stripping back of all my previous capacities."

"Every three months I hit a wall that produced feelings of wanting to go back to being a high-functioning person instead speaking like a five-year-old and needing guidance for everything from buying floor soap to shampoo. I had to entrust my passport with a good friend so I wouldn't leave the country at those times."

"No clear role and no ability to see how I was contributing in any way to those around me."

"Figuring out what was actually expected of me. This may have been related to team dynamics, but I always felt like I wasn't doing enough or that I was doing everything wrong, but I also felt like I was listening to the Holy Spirit. It was tough to navigate that."

Reading their responses, I am struck by the range of messages. Messages of being too young, too white, too rich, too culturally slow, too uninformed, too much like deadweight, too stupid, too you-fill-in-the-blank. Maybe you have received similar messages of "too something." Want to know why they sting so much? Because often they are "good" lies. A "bad" lie is easy to dismiss since it does not sound believable. If you told me Erin did not love me, I would not believe you. I knew she loved me. But why can I remember hearing, in vivid detail, "Amy is loud and maybe a bit too much" when students said, "Amy, you are outgoing!" Combining my boisterous personality with memories of my sisters rolling their eyes at me when I would tell stories from my job—"Oh no, not another hamburger story!"—resulted in a message that I was too much. Now, here

I was on the other side of the world, in a very different context, and when I heard "outgoing," I interpreted it as "loud and too much." It was the lie the Accuser of my soul whispered, and because I feared it to be true, I believed him.

Over time I have grown in my awareness that this is the quicksand he likes to trap me in, but even just yesterday I found myself believing a version of this very same lie. The Accuser will use the lies you believe about yourself and masquerade them as the truth to try to trap you. While every one of us will face these types of messages, one group of people on the field seems to face them more than others. We turn to that role next.

A Word for the One Who May Be Overlooked

I want to take a moment and talk to the stay-at-home spouses who might not have a designated role. Your experience with role deprivation will be influenced by your personal history, organization, and host country. Many an organization considers both spouses to be employees and equally sent out. However, the type of work you do will influence the type of visa you get, which will impact your legal designation for tax purposes. For instance, are you on a work visa, a student visa, or a tourist visa? Glamourous, I know. But understanding your organization might be audited by the government where they are registered, your organization may need to have terminology that will keep them compliant with the laws and employment regulations.

While this makes sense, it can lead to terminology that can take concerns you already have and add gasoline to the confusion. For example, my friends Jack and Diane. In

America, Jack was a pastor and Diane was a stay-at-home mom of their three kids. However, in China Jack was not able to be the TIC "employee" because he did not have a degree the visa-issuing part of the government would accept. So, Diane, who had an MA in education, taught English to Chinese college students and Jack stayed home with their kids. Diane enjoyed teaching enough, but she really wanted to be home with the children, and Jack wanted to teach English to the college students. In their case, after a year in the country, they explored other roles within the organization. Over time Jack earned an MA online, allowing him to be granted a work visa legally, and started teaching English as he had dreamed about.

Another friend, Sally, worked full-time as a pharmacist and loved working outside the home. The organization Sally and her family moved to Asia with didn't allow her to work outside the home, at least not the first year; since her husband was the official employee, she would need to stay home and educate their children. The transition from working outside the house full-time work to staying home full-time was bumpy. Not only did her role change, but they lived where winter lasted for months, which made it virtually impossible for the kids to play outside most of the year. How about that role of "trapped-indoors stay-at-home mom"? You might not be trapped by the weather, but you might understand why year one was extra challenging for Sally as she watched her husband, Brian, thrive in his new role, and desired to thrive in her new roles too.

Too often the terminology used to describe you can be cringeworthy when it comes to placing value on your role.

I asked people on Facebook what terms they have heard used to describe people in your situation, and this is the list people provided:

- Nonteaching spouse
- Trailing spouse
- Support spouse
- Accompanying spouse
- Home and family support
- The "so-what-do-you-do-with-your-time?" spouse (This was followed by the laughing-with-tears emoji and given more likes, loves, and ha-ha responses than any other comment.)
- Reluctant spouse
- "M" wife/spouse
- Cross-cultural worker
- Home evangelist
- Gilded cage
- A plus-one type of scenario

As my Facebook friends discussed this, one said, "'Trailing' spouse gives a connotation that the spouse may not be pleased to be there. I am not the employee—which frankly has some benefits—but yet we are entirely in this member care position together. In reality, we are partners in ministry, we need both of us to do this big job. So maybe there is a distinction between outside perception and self-perception of the label? Or sometimes the label leads to personal perception? Just a thought." What an excellent point to make.

You might be in your sweet spot in your current context,

and although experiencing adjustment you are cool with your role. However, if you are wrestling a bit—or are in an MMA-style fight—with yourself or God over your position this year, I promise, you are not the only one. Here is what one survey participant said she would tell her first-year self: "You are not the employee, your husband is. Take a step back and grieve (and enjoy) this moment for what it is. God is showing you something new, about Himself and about you. (Also, you will survive)."

Another participant, when asked what she learned about herself, said, "My identity was wrapped up in my accomplishments as a working mom who also served in youth ministry alongside my husband. But I shifted to staying at home with our daughter and learning a new lifestyle of not getting much done but discovering the value of being with my daughter."

Finding your place will take time. If it helps, you have permission to give yourself a role and even a title. When I look at Jesus, He experienced role deprivation as He went from one role to another. You too, like every human on the planet, were created with a desire for meaningful ways to contribute and participate. Maybe your role this year is "home establisher." Or maybe you will be the "market expert" on your team, visiting the local market every week with an eye for noticing something new. Perhaps you will be the "prayer warrior" and spend consistent time in prayer for the requests of the team. Whatever it may be, your role is important, no matter who notices or doesn't notice; whether it has a given title, one you made up, or no title at all—each role is important.

Lastly, I recommend you chart your role. Find a way to record—daily or weekly—how you helped to establish your home, added to your market knowledge, or prayed. Role deprivation is real; however, it does not have to become a black hole for you. In the discouraging moments you can then look at what you've recorded and remind yourself that your new role still matters, even when it doesn't feel or seem like it.

Let Love Root You

If you read *Looming Transitions*, a book I wrote to prepare cross-cultural workers to transition to or from the field, you know I wrote about accepting the tension that comes with transitions. Tension exists because simultaneously parts of you are ending while new parts of you are just beginning. Tension also exists because you want to keep your soul fertile, and that involves allowing parts of you to die so that new parts can be born.[16] When a transition is no longer looming and you are now on the field, part of keeping your soul fertile is awareness. Awareness of the kind of person you want to be. Awareness that it is possible to let certain parts die and plant new ones. Awareness that fertile can look fallow on the surface. Awareness that it is hard to wait for parts of yourself to be born, but it is necessary. Awareness that you may need to start afresh to stay you. Awareness that while a fertile soul may not be the heart cry of the world, it is the heart cry of God. He loves you and cares more about being *with* you on this journey than *where* you have landed.[17]

---

16 Donald Miller, *Through Painted Deserts: Light, God, and Beauty on the Open Road* (Nashville, TN: Thomas Nelson Publishers, 2005), x.
17 Amy Young, *Looming Transitions: Starting Well and Finishing Well in Cross-Cultural Service*, (Charlotte: CreateSpace, 2016), 12.

As you might be painfully aware, after a part of you dies, the new part rarely springs immediately into place. If you landed in an ideal situation (praise God, it *can* happen), enjoy it and every so often remind yourself to remain grateful. For some of you, you will find your footing over the year. But for others, your first year might look like a barren field. When asked about the hardest part of the first year, one survey response simply said, "Loss of identity." The sparseness of the response says it all.

Ultimately role deprivation is one of the tender ways Jesus identifies with us: "rather, He made himself nothing by taking the very nature of a servant, being made in human likeness" (Philippians 2:7). Jesus knows what it is like to lay aside a role in obedience to His father. Paul and other New Testament authors do not go into detail about how Jesus navigated role deprivation and the limits that came with it, but we do know that Jesus faithfully took time on His own to be with God. I wonder if part of His time was spent with God reminding Him how much His father loved Him. When I am secure (aware of my belovedness), I am less likely to need a role to define me.

Dallas Willard said this regarding 1 Corinthians 13: "Paul is not primarily giving instructions on how Christians should live, but describing what God is like. First and foremost, these words describe God's love, a love that is the fruit of God's absolute self-sufficiency. The key to loving like this is to be 'filled with all the fullness of God' (Eph. 3:19)."[18] First

---

18 Dallas Willard, *Life Without Lack: Living the Fullness of Psalm 23* (Nashville, TN: Thomas Nelson, 2018), Kindle location 1024.

Corinthians 13 has become hijacked by familiarity. Honestly, it is so familiar I can go on autopilot when it comes up. *Love is patient . . . yeah, yeah, I know.* (Yes, I do realize how ironic that is.)

Once, though not in my first year, a colleague asked our team to pray through 1 Corinthians 13 regarding a relational situation the team was going through. I was so stirred up over what was happening that I thought, *Why not, I think we are near rock bottom, it can't hurt.* I prayed for my colleagues and the situation until God interrupted me with this whispered question. "Amy, what would it look like to love yourself this way?"

Even though I was sitting in a chair, I felt a bit shaky because it had never occurred to me that the passage could apply to how I love myself. Instead, I had read, studied, and prayed about love—when I wasn't on autopilot—in relation to how I could love others. In that tender moment, the phrase "love is kind" shimmered, and the Holy Spirit asked what I could do in the situation that was kind to myself. This wasn't really so much about me being kind to me but about being reminded of how much God loves me. During this difficult season He reminded me that He was not merely using me to love my teammates but that He saw how messy it was, how hard it had become, and how fatigued I was. *Love is kind.* I really heard it this time—and I wept.

As a minister of God's love to your local friends, your teammates, and your family, this year you will also need to be a minister of God's love to you. Though we can always be loving toward ourselves, this year you will need to be more consciously kind to yourself than in other seasons of your life.

Role deprivation is messy, at times hard, and, as the weeks turn into months, draining. You prepared for your time on the field with a sincere and earnest heart to love and serve the people you have come to live amongst. As I have stressed, this year is unique. You won't always feel the way you do now. So when the twinge, or perhaps a two-by-four to the head, of role deprivation springs up this year, remind yourself that God is love and He did not bring you here merely to use you for Him. He also brought you here to love you.

One survey response sums up the route cross-cultural workers often go through in regard to the incarnational process, role deprivation, and love: "I think one of the biggest things I learned was that I had unwittingly allowed my identity to be shaped by the relationships that I had in my life. When those relationships and my status as a known and loved teacher were stripped away, I had to figure out where my worth lay. I had to come to the place where I trusted that Jesus saw me, knew me, and loved me even if no one else in my daily world really did."

If 1 Corinthians 13 is more about God's nature and the nature of love than marching orders, receive this as God's nature and His love for you:

> Love is patient with you when you don't know yet what your role is.
> Love is kind when you make a cultural faux pas.
> Love does not envy when others catch on faster or have a more definite role.
> It does not boast by covering up the insecurity and unsureness you feel.
> It is not proud when your children are better behaved than your teammates' kids.

It does not dishonor others (or yourself).

It is not self-seeking because it is secure not in what it does but whose it is.

It is not easily angered when you cannot remember new words after studying them.

It keeps no record of wrongs, such as when you were cheated buying fruit because you are the "rich foreigner."

Love does not delight in evil but rejoices in the truth of how beloved you are.

Love always protects, always trusts, always hopes, always perseveres.

Love never fails.

What a picture. If you need a mantra this first year, try out "God in His love always protects me, always trusts, always hopes in me, and always perseveres."

As Dallas Willard reminds us, "At the center of so many of our difficulties is fear—fear of rejection, fear of failure, fear of death, fear of sickness, fear of not being able to take care of ourselves in old age, fear of what may happen to our loved ones. There are so many things that frighten us. What is the answer to all of our fears? Love. The love that comes out of plentitude—out of the fulness of God's sufficiency."[19]

When you feel a sense of lacking and you wonder what your role is this first year, remind yourself that your main purpose is to learn to let God love you more than you did before you arrived on the field. If God's love for you is pervasive in this first year, it will change the rest of your life. When you are

---

19 Willard, *Life Without Lack*, Kindle location 1029.

secure in your belovedness, roles can come and go without the need to cling to the parts of you that are going to change with time for the better. When it happens, and it will, you'll be able to walk through the invisible pudding with love.

5
Torn Between Worlds

Oh, that every step to the field was scattered with deep thoughts, Scripture references, and angelic reactions. Instead, this popped into my head: "You have got to be kidding me." I realized the day I would leave for pre-field training was my mom's birthday. Because I moved to China in my mid- to late twenties, what was exciting and teeming with life for me was agony for my parents, especially my mom. My parents have been supportive of me from day one even when I was the kid who applied to college six hundred miles away. And here we were, nine years after I flew the nest for college, punctuating just how far away I would go out in the world by leaving on her birthday. Obedience to Jesus helped my parents with my roaming—okay, not removing the pain of my leaving but at least explaining the reason for it.

Leaving any other day, I might have underestimated how much my call would cost my family. How much my call would have us forever calculating time zones and lugging packages to the post office. How often I would miss—and be missed at—weddings, births, holidays, big games won by my sports team, and uncountable ordinary moments. How much God's call would begin to mean I would feel the tug of two worlds for the rest of my life and my family would have the tug of me living in two worlds.

Arriving at the airport, Dad and I unloaded two of the largest suitcases on the planet and enough carry-on luggage for a small village to set up base camp, setting them on the sidewalk. We hugged at the curb, trying to stifle tears so that the goodbye would not be even more painful. My dad walked around the car to the driver's side and opened the door, smiling at me one last time before he got in. Mom opened her door and, making good on her promise to God to prepare me for the world, waved me off to the other side of it. I turned and walked into the airport, struggling through my tears to read the signs for the check-in counter while also feeling relieved that the final goodbye Band-Aid was ripped off. For me, the adventure of cross-cultural service was finally beginning; for my friends and family, the reality of life with an Amy-sized-hole had just begun.

After a month of pre-field training in California, a one-day travel delay (seriously?!), and a few days of touring in Beijing with our school officials, Erin and I finally arrived at our new home. My journal entry begins, "We're here!" and goes on to explain how the head school official (*waiban*, one of our first Chinese words) met us at the airport and helped settle us in our apartments. In my journal, I was already having trouble capturing our living arrangements in a way that would make sense to others. As I mentioned earlier, our two apartments consisted of four hotel rooms with Erin and me sharing a kitchen and living room in my (our?) and one of Erin's (my?) apartment being a junk room where we stored luggage and things we did not use regularly (See how confusing it is to describe?). On that first night, my impression was, "Our living conditions are excellent and the bathtubs look brand new." We were left alone because it was late in the evening and told to go to bed.

A few minutes later a knock on the door brought our first visitor, the dean of the English Department; greeting me with a cheerful warning to "mind my doors because Chengdu is famous for mice." According to my journal he had a lovely British accent. Funny what stands out when everything is new. I got up the next morning at 7:30 a.m. (I am struck by how often, in my Americanness, I recorded the time of events) noting that my bed did not have sheets nor my room air conditioning. Instead of what I would call sheets, my bed had giant towels, one over the mattress and another to cover me. Each bedroom had an oscillating fan, so, as my journal says, "the nights are not too bad."

Mr. Xu, the head *waiban*, was to come over at 10:00 a.m. for a meeting. "However, at 8:30 a.m. the doorbell rang, and there was Mr. Xu who was ready to take us on a walking tour of the area." After the walking tour, we returned to our apartment for the meeting. "When Mr. Xu started the meeting by saying 'Chengdu is in the south (pointing down) west (pointing left) part of China,' I knew we were in for a long meeting." And it was. The afternoon was dedicated to figuring out how to use our washing machine, a "two-hour adventure" because of all of the refilling, draining, and spinning. "But our clothes are clean and, with the help of the fan, on their way to drying."

That evening the school hosted a welcoming banquet for us. "Erin wanted to laugh because we were expected to dress up for the banquet, but all of the college officials showed up in their shorts. During the entire meal, no one talked to me, which I thought was odd. It was more like we were an excuse for all these men to get together and have a fancy meal. The president of the college kept blowing his nose on the floor! I ate an eel dish that made my mouth go numb and several of the dishes were very odd; but they did not force us to eat anything we didn't want. Glad to have it over and done with and that they gave us leftovers!"[20]

After the banquet, Mark and his friend Steve came over. (Does it add to the story that they arrived at 7:10? Oh, Amy, your time obsession is a bit nutty.) Since Mark had taught at our school the year before, we "bombarded [him] with questions about the classes, gifts we brought, who had visited, classes, cultural lectures, and classes." Teaching being high on our stress scale. Erin tried to call her mom after they left and couldn't get through, "so I decided to call home collect. It was 7:30 a.m. in Colorado and Mom was the only one home. She kept freaking out that I had called her and wondered if everything was all right. You'd think I'd never been here before! Ha. She was getting ready to have breakfast with [her friend] Susan and was going to call Dad to tell him we had

---

[20] I cringed rereading this and even started to editorialize and explain how much I *clearly* did not understand the culture. Of course I didn't know much! I could still count the number of days I had been in the country on one hand. Allow your first-year self to be who he or she is, first-year you, for you cannot know what five- or twenty-year you will know. If it were not for first-year Amy, I would have forgotten that the president blew his nose on the ground. Thank you, first-year Amy, for writing about him; and girl, you will always love that eel dish, and you will come to understand banquet etiquette so much better. What I am trying to say is, thank you for not censoring yourself.

arrived. An excellent day, but we are excited for the weekend when we will be left alone to get settled in our apartments."

Thus began the adventure for me, complete with visitors, mice, laundry, banquets, eel, nose blowing, and trying to get our footing for the classes we would start on Monday. Even in the early journal entries you get an inkling of what this experience was like for my family as they were learning to live half a world away from me. When you follow God's call your friends and families end up experiencing the adjustment more than is generally acknowledged.

It All Depends

Because I was relatively young, had made an initial two-year commitment (translation, "only" two years, not a prolonged separation), and did not have any major drama or family crises in the first year, my journal is devoid of many instances of missing people or places. However, my journal gives a detailed account of each activity I did every day and of course the time I did it. On occasion, I noted when I got a letter from home, and only once in the first six months did I write that I sobbed after reading a letter from my sister. Around the end of November, as the weather changed and we had no break for American Thanksgiving, my journal still sounds like I am in the midst of a great adventure for Jesus.

When else would you run in a relay race for the English Department on Thanksgiving? Being significantly larger than most of the people from southern China, I should say, *when else do you get to humiliate yourself in front of a massive crowd?* Erin, Mark, and I went to a Beijing duck restaurant for Thanksgiving dinner and brought a small can of cranberry sauce.

Beijing duck on Thanksgiving?! Come on, you cannot make this stuff up; I was living the dream.

"The family called at 6:15 Friday morning which was just after lunch (or should I say Thanksgiving dinner). It was the first time I talked with my sister Laura since August! They passed the phone around and the best time was when Elizabeth, Laura, and I were joking around." That is what I had to say about missing my first major holiday—the first holiday, in fact, where my family of origin was not together. No musings over what my family ate, what I was missing, or how choked up I was hearing their voices. Reading it now, I am struck by what I did not record because it already felt normal. The only phone available was at the front desk of the hotel I lived in; I did not record that I hung on every word while other hotel guests listened to my call.

Since my friends were young professionals, most of their letters to me were about their jobs, their churches, or their social lives. A few days after Thanksgiving I wrote, "I got a letter from [my dear friend] Amy, and she's pregnant! And I am the first to know. I think I'll try and call her next week." Her letter marks another first, the first significant life change to a friend or family member that I would miss. But it also felt expected, as Amy and Bill had been married for several years, he was nearing the end of his PhD program, and a child seemed the next logical step. I was more excited than sad.

When the Angel of Death Lands
Unfortunately, your first year might come with trauma instead of engagements, weddings, and birth announcements. One surprise finding from the survey was how many people

experienced the death of a family member during their first year. I do not wish a traumatic event upon you or your family, but if we do not speak directly about what could happen your first year, you are even more unprepared for the possibility. Most importantly, if it does happen, I want you to know you're in good company.

These survey comments let you see the deaths of participants' loved ones in the fuller context of their first-year experiences:

"I gave my year a seven on a scale of one to ten because I had an excellent time, but also my mom got cancer, had major surgery, and my aunt and grandpa both died."

"My dad died as I was getting ready to go to field training. It was a hard year being away from family after his death."

"The first six months were awful. My dad died one month after I got here and I returned home for three weeks. Then came back to the field with grief to a horrible case of culture shock."

"It was full of disasters: repeated malaria, my non-Christian mum's unexpected death, poor work relationships, moving home on average every six weeks, a job I did not like; total lack of understanding/support from colleagues after Mum died; I felt I was constantly failing and not measuring up to the organization's apparent standards and work ethic."

"Although life was very exciting, I missed my children away at university and my mother died unexpectedly, so I had a lot to deal with. Overall, though, we had been well prepared and the school that had hired us was good at helping us through the transition."

"What ended up being the hardest was my brother dying (hardly usual but it does happen). Also hard was the kids' struggle fitting in, which they did but it takes time, and at the end of our first year I felt like everyone I had gotten close to left unexpected and with unclear reasons."

I added up the family members reported in the survey to have died: eleven family members died during a cross-cultural worker's first year, roughly six percent of those who responded to the survey. The death of a family member while you are on the field is hard. I once prayed a teammate through an international flight in hopes that she would arrive in time to say goodbye in person. But navigating the death of a loved one in your first year, while you are still adjusting to a new culture as well as trying to make a good impression on people you have known only for a short period, is traumatic.

Six years after I moved to China I became the Member Care Director for my organization, and part of my job entailed meeting new teachers in California and spending a week with them during pre-field orientation before their orientation continued in China. I always flew back to Beijing a couple days before them so that they would have one familiar face greet them when they emerged from customs, jet-lagged and with mounds of luggage. One year, as the new teachers were nearing the end of their orientation in Beijing and would be leaving in just a few days for their assigned schools, Katherine's roommate called me and asked me to come to their room.

Katherine was lying in bed, clearly in shock. Her roommate explained that Katherine had just gotten off the phone with family, who had informed her that her uncle was found brutally murdered in his kitchen. After sharing this news, her roommate left. I sat on the floor next to her bed, and took a moment for the information to sink in. Murdered? What? This was not the first time I was helping a cross-cultural worker process and respond to a family member's death, but it was my first (and only) murder. Katherine was assigned to a four-person team; one other gal was also new to the field, and her two other teammates had been at their school for several years.

She needed to decide quickly whether to go to her school with her teammates or return to the US for her uncle's funeral. Her uncle had not been close to the family; she understood that by leaving for a few weeks she would put stress on her teammates. What would they think of her? God was sovereign and she trusted He would meet her in this decision, but that did not help her in-shock brain know what she should do.

Though the decision was mostly hers, I knew TIC would support her the best we could whatever she decided and that her school would understand the unusual nature of her situation. Since we were only talking about a few weeks and she had the means to return home, she decided to be with her family. Katherine later ended up staying on the field for several years and then worked in TIC's headquarters even longer. She told me that TIC's response, her teammates' support, and her family's ability to be together for a few weeks allowed her to stay on the field and remain in full-time ministry for years. Each situation is unique, and there is no "one size fits all" response to death, but my hope and prayer is that if you experience the death of a loved one this year, you, too, will be loved and supported.

Cuts Hurt
Let's review: we jumped from my first Thanksgiving, in which I did not seem to miss my family as much as I expected, to a family member murdered in his kitchen. Well, now can you say, "Extreme examples, Amy!?" Chances are your reality will be less extreme than either bliss or murder. You will not know if your first year is going to be one fun adventure for Jesus after another or one painful situation for Jesus after another until you are in the middle of it. But you do know this: no matter what, you will still be torn because you cannot be in two places at once.

This sense of being torn came up in the survey responses too:

"Our first year was hard on our kids. It was tough to see your five-year-old daughter fall asleep crying as she hugged a photo of her grandparents."

"Dealing with family stuff back home. I think being away from family in the stressful moments was hard, and not being able to do anything about it. It was made even worse by the eight-hour time difference, and I would wake up to entire email conversations that I couldn't take part in."

"Distance from friends and family during extreme illness

(mine and theirs) was one of the hardest parts."
"One of the hardest parts was missing home. I missed belonging, my family, my school, and my church. I missed being available to grieve the loss of a former student with people who knew her and were feeling the same pain and sadness I was. I missed sharing major life changes with my friends. It was hard to feel like I didn't belong anywhere—I wasn't accepted or trusted in this new place yet, but my old world was moving on without me."

In response to what survey participants would tell their first-year selves, people wrote:

"You are doing great, and when the moments of being sad over what you've left come, don't push them away. Every time you are homesick, thank God for that item you miss and His goodness."

"You might not experience culture shock. You will be surprised by how normal this foreign life starts to feel after a while (maybe months, maybe a year). It won't always seem so different. You won't always miss people back home so fiercely it hurts. Trust Him. Trust Him, trust Him, trust Him."

Watching your kids suffer, seeing life move on "back home," trying to help with family stuff from a distance, knowing you do not yet belong, experiencing homesickness, missing people to the point it hurts—all examples of the ways you can be torn between worlds. Some of these cuts are deep; some are more like paper cuts, but even paper cuts distract and hurt. No one gets a pass on ever being pulled in different directions, not even those who are called by God. In thinking about this section of the book, I studied four people in the Bible—Joseph, Sarah, Hannah, and Moses—who also experienced separation from those they loved. I was struck by the details included in their stories.

Joseph, as you know, is sold into slavery in his youth, experiencing more ups and downs than a roller coaster as he meets Potiphar, Potiphar's wife, the jailer, the cupbearer, the baker, and even Pharaoh himself. Finally, his life lands on a smooth section, and he is instrumental in preparing Egypt for the famine, stockpiling food for seven years before it hit. The Bible does not say how many years into the famine he first sees his brothers. We know that Joseph is thirty when "he enter[s] the service of Pharaoh king of Egypt" and that at least seven years pass before his brothers arrive (Genesis 41:46–47). So Joseph is probably in his late thirties when his brothers show up wanting to buy grain. Though it has been about twenty years since he saw them, he recognizes them immediately. Is this any surprise? When you return home for your first visit, you, too, will scan the waiting area until your eyes land in recognition on your loved ones.

For Joseph it is not yet time to tell them who he is. He waits until his brothers are desperate enough for food that they return with his brother Benjamin. Eventually it the time comes for the grand reveal. Note the first question out of his mouth: "I am Joseph! Is my father still living?" (Genesis 45:3). Though a grown man, married, a father himself, and employed with a position of great power, he still feels the separation from family.

Joseph is not the only one who lived long periods separated from family. Sarai (later Sarah) leaves her family in Ur to travel with her husband and his family to Harran. In Harran God calls Abraham to "go from your country, your people and your father's household to the land I will show you" (Genesis 12:1). After years of infertility, Sarai will no longer have the support of family or steady community as her infertility continues. Instead, she faces famine (the reason they went to Egypt) and so many moves I got lost studying Genesis, trying to track their journeys on a map. Eventually the angels visit Abraham and Sarah in Mamre, promising that within a year she will have a child. Sarah knows what it is like when your heart is torn amid a life of calling.

Or take Hannah who only sees her son once a year when the family travels to Shiloh for the annual sacrifice. While the Bible records how wicked Eli's sons are—the NIV describes them as scoundrels, talk about juicy details—Samuel is reported as "ministering before the LORD—a boy wearing a linen ephod. Each year his mother made him a little robe and took it to him when she went up with her husband to offer the annual sacrifice" (1 Samuel 2:18–19). Picture Hannah choosing the material, cutting it out, and sewing love into every stitch of his new robe. The anticipation building as she packs her bag and starts the trek toward her son, knowing their time together will fly. Hannah is eager to see how he has grown in a year. Loving Samuel as much as her other children, even though their time in person is limited. Hannah knows what it is like to see a loved one for only a short period.

One final example involves three generations. Moses meets his wife, Zipporah, when he escapes to Midian; they marry and start a family. Roughly forty years pass when God calls Moses to return to Egypt and Jethro, Moses's father-in-law, encourages him, "Go, and I wish you well" (Exodus 4:18). Oh, that all parents would bless their child's call. Ten plagues later, after one parting of the Red Sea, a drowned army, learning to eat manna from heaven and drink water from a rock, and having defeated the Amalekites, Jethro can visit the family.

Just as if your family is able to visit, Jethro spends time with Moses, observing his setup. Based on what he sees, he asks Moses why he judges the people the way that he does. Moses's answer is honest and shows that he doesn't have a compelling reason. Jethro shoots straight with his son-in-law: "What you are doing is not good. You and these people who come to you will only wear yourselves out" (Exodus 18:17–18). Wisely, "Moses listened to his father-in-law and did everything he said" (Exodus 18:24).

You might not be able to have family visit you this year in person (actually, I would recommend no visitors this first year). But one of the losses you experience your first year is going from a supportive environment where everyone knows you and can give you feedback. You might be like Moses and be so close to your life, even with a new community, that you cannot objectively see what is working and what is not serving you well. Allow people the right to speak into your life. Not everyone is safe or wise, but some are. Let the safe and wise in.

Joseph was separated from an aging parent, Sarah from a consistent community, Hannah unable to watch a child she loves on a regular basis, and Moses was without the wisdom of a trusted voice in his life. God included their details because being torn between worlds is a tale as old as time. Be encouraged that God sees you too.

Even David Was Lonely
You are going to be lonely and tempted to think that others are not as lonely as you are. Singles will be tempted to believe their married teammates cannot be lonely because they have each other. (And sex. People who have sex are less lonely than people who don't, right?) Marrieds will be tempted to believe their single teammates cannot be as lonely as they are because they have more time to go out and interact with people. (And freedom. People with more freedom are less lonely than people tied to family responsibilities, right?)

Wrong.

Sex. Freedom. Children. Teammates. Language skills. Great housing. Fast internet. Being an introvert. Being an extrovert. Being an ambivert. Loving the culture. Hating the culture. Nothing can prevent you from being lonely in your first year.

As this survey participant said, loneliness will find you:

"I was feeling so alone and stupid for not knowing anything about the ministry on our field. Adjustments take time (I know) but I was expecting to learn and fit in quickly when the other cross-cultural workers talked about their work. I really wanted to track with them but couldn't even distinguish between their talking about people and places. I was in Indonesia, and they also use many acronyms like words. Plus, our field had people from more than just our US-based organization, so I was learning multiple culture cues at the same time. I did learn eventually, but that first year was very lonely at times."

Notice how often loneliness was listed as one of the hardest parts of the first year:

"My expectations were smashed, I had issues with my organization, and experienced deep loneliness."

"Team, team, team (and loneliness and finances and culture 'confusion' and supporters!)"

"Loneliness: not having local friends, a spouse, or a roommate."

"Loneliness, conflict with teammates, loss of identity."

"Loneliness/homesickness, conflict with other expats, communication with sending organization."

"Team conflict, loneliness, and learning how to do business transactions."

The word "loneliness" ricochets through these answers.

Participants did not mince words, did they? Neither did David when he wrote, "Turn to me and be gracious to me, for I am lonely and afflicted. Relieve the troubles of my heart and free me from my anguish" (Psalm 25:16–17). The best advice I can give to you is not to try and "lonely-proof" your life. Every stage of life comes with its own variety of feeling alone and has a sense of a lack of belonging. You can be proactive and look for ways to soften or lessen some loneliness because this is different from proofing, but you won't eliminate it altogether.

Start with a short inventory of when you have felt lonely in the past. Do you notice any triggers? For me, if I sensed I was on the verge of a pity party and my defenses were down, I learned it was not wise to watch sports movies. Sports movies triggered the sense that my people were on the other side of the world and able to watch sports together. Poor me, I was in China, by myself, and would never ever get to watch a sporting event with anyone else who actually cares about the game and I would never be able to celebrate a Super Bowl or NCAA championship victory with anyone in China. The call of God came with a price too high to pay, and I was paying it in missed opportunities galore! Galore, I say! You can see how my inner conversation spiraled down. Usually I could watch sports movies and feel encouraged about life and sports, proud to be a part of the human race, but I learned I needed to avoid them whenever I was feeling lonely.

You, too, will have apps, movies, or songs that are typically no problem for you. But when you are down, they become a gateway to exacerbating your loneliness.

Know your triggers, because if you don't, they can own you. Set up a system ahead of time to let teammates or prayer supporters know to pray for you. During a pity party or when you find yourself at the bottom of an emotional well, you will not feel like making a plan. You will feel like eating forty-seven cookies, or punching someone in the face, or lying on your couch watching the latest game or must-see TV show. While you can soften loneliness, you cannot avoid it. In those moments, instead of trying to run faster than loneliness, let it wash over you. Like David, cry out to God and ask him to be gracious to you. He will. That person you think is having lots of sex or making local friends with all of their free time? They may turn out to be lonely, too, and want to go out for noodles.

You Cannot Live in Four States at One Time
On a road trip when I was a kid, we visited a tourist site called the Four Corners. The boundaries of four states meet and form a giant plus sign. So you can have your left foot in Arizona, your right foot in New Mexico, your left hand in Utah, your right hand in Colorado, and your behind high in the air.

While you can *be* in four states at one time, you cannot *live* in four at one time—you have to pick one. Technology may try to fool you that you can avoid the pain of being torn, inviting you to invest equally in two worlds. You will have to choose which world you will live in—and which you will merely check in with. You can still be invested in and care about people back home, but ultimately this year, as you feel untethered, make small choices to anchor you to your new world.

As this survey participant said, "You cannot expect to live in two worlds at once. Dig in with both feet and get involved. Remember that people at home have a hole in their lives where you used to fit, but life goes on and they need to fill the hole. That does not mean they don't miss you and won't accept you when you do come home, but things will never be the same."

6
God and You

The school I taught at provided and furnished my first apartment in China. I told you a bit about it earlier and said it was hard to describe. Though nothing fancy, it was more than adequate. The school owned the small hotel on campus and had converted four first-floor rooms into two apartments. My apartment consisted of two hotel rooms that were joined by knocking out the wall between the enclosed balconies. Erin and I joked we had a two-butt kitchen because a small sink and a two-burner stove were installed at one end of the balcony, just enough room for one of us to be doing dishes and the other cooking. The other end of the balcony held a cupboard for our dishes and food from care packages. The "dining room"—aka second hotel room—came complete with a sturdy folding table, four folding chairs, a large wall mirror, the smallest refrigerator I had seen outside of a college door room, a toaster oven that became our most beloved kitchen appliance, a bookcase, and two Mao chairs.

If you have seen a formal picture of Chinese government officials with the front row seated, hands formally posed on the arms of the chairs, and the second row of officials standing behind them, you have seen a Mao chair. In offices across China it was standard to see two Mao chairs, named after

GETTING STARTED

Chairman Mao, with a small table in between them. Though I moved to China a good two decades after Mao died, I am fairly certain he could have sat in our chairs because their days of being comfortable, if they ever existed, were long gone. The chairs were so uncomfortable and formal we finally moved one ninety degrees so we could see each other during team meetings and not feel that we were in a government meeting during prayer times.

Mark often came to our apartment, and we three thought of ourselves as unofficial teammates, so it was natural for Mark to join us for church. When I dig through my memories and try to uncover what I anticipated church would look like in China, I knew that we would not often go to a public church. Because few public churches existed and China had strong norms about how to treat foreigners, we would always be the guests and be given a seat as a sign of honor. I could not bear the thought that a faithful grandma or grandpa of the faith who had waited in line for a seat would be shooed out so that I could sit. Thus, I pictured myself rarely attending a formal church. Looking back I can see that I forgot to imagine what we *would do* for church.

So three people, a guitar, and a book about the Psalms sounded like, honestly, nothing I had experienced and did not fit into the category "church." Church was planned and executed by others, and by others I mean pastors and church staff, not three of us in the "congregation." When I look back at my journal from my first few weeks, I recorded Sunday as days for lesson planning, lounging, and cooking. A month in I wrote, "Mark came over and we made pancakes—had to go and buy eggs and milk. He was frustrated with how the first few turned out, but after that, they were great. Erin and I cooked apples, made lemon Jell-O, and peeled off more of the stickers the previous tenants put on the windows. Cooking actually took a while and we ate around 1:00 p.m. Absolutely delicious. Sang praises. Awesome to have a twelve-string guitar, no less! We decided to study the book of Psalms, and through drawing lots, I am the lucky first leader."

Apparently, complete sentences were too much of a hassle. Ha! But look at how much space I gave to food compared to the church part of the morning. I do not recall pre-field orientation mentioning casting lots as a way to make team decisions, but there you have it. We started meeting every Sunday morning for church. Because Mark could play the guitar and loved music, we always had worship songs. I do not doubt that God received our singing as a beautiful offering, but I remember feeling that it was anything but. Three normal voices are three normal voices, no matter how "holy" our endeavors to make a joyful noise. Trio greatness was not our destiny.

Though I grew to love the intimacy of a smaller group, no place exists to hide when it is just three of you. As I mentioned in the introduction, the impetus for this book started with a comment from Lisa, an online Velvet Ashes small group member. Offhandedly Lisa said that when she moved to Africa, she had not realized how responsible she would be for her relationship with God on the field. The ah-ha may have been inaudible, her comment clicking a truth into place in my mind: your relationship with God changes when you move to the field because you are responsible for it in ways you do not have to be when you are in your home country.

By the end of this chapter, if your takeaway is a version

of "Understood. Buy more devotionals, download more sermons. Got it," I have failed to communicate the heart and the gift this year offers you. The simple reality is that most of us come from situations where it is easy to access God, as much as accessing the Maker of Heaven and Earth can be said to be easy. Likely, your relationship with God pre-field was nurtured through regular church attendance in a language you understood, coupled with some form of church or ministry involvement, spiritual practices, and deep in-person relationships. In this context, you knew how to feed yourself. You had annual rhythms and knew how to pace yourself. You had people to turn to in a pinch.

Over time you will have these in place, but during your first year you might not have the language or be in a context where it is safe or wise to attend a public church. Likewise, it often takes time for ministry opportunities to get up and running. On the other hand, your start on the field may fall closer to the other extreme, and you may become overwhelmed with ministry involvement in a new context. Whether eager to dive in or trying to avoid being overwhelmed, you will still have to find ways to worship and be spiritually fed.

The Gift, the Responsibility, and the Promise

The paradox of cross-cultural work is that what you do is vital but can appear rather insignificant on any given day. This year presents you with the opportunity to practice holding on to both truths that what you do is important and may also feel insignificant. God will work through you, but you are not a mere tool in God's toolbox for this location. God was here long before your visa was granted, and even if you are here for decades, He will be here after you go. God loves you and sees you and brought you here to serve and to grow. When it comes to your relationship with God as you adjust to the field, picture it like a tryptic with the left panel holding a gift, the center panel revealing a responsibility, and the right panel reminding you of a promise.

The Gift
I've mentioned before that a fertile soul requires that things die in order to create space for new things to grow. Your life may look like an empty field. The gift of this year is time to reflect and evaluate. Resist the urge to fill up your days too quickly. And while I sound like a broken record about how much time daily life will take, it will not take all of your time. As the year goes on, your life will fill up with friends and conversations will become deeper. However, for the first few months, you might want to bang your head against the wall at having the same seemingly inane discussions. I remember saying to Erin after a couple months, "Is it too much to ask to have one deep conversation with someone other than with you and Mark?!" Let the boredom of this year set patterns and rhythms in place that will position you for the long haul. Use the following questions either monthly or quarterly throughout the first year. By looking at them multiple times over the months, you will see what changes and what remains constant.

1. Reflect on what you enjoyed prior to moving to the field about your friends, finances, spiritual life, work, health, and investing in people.
2. What was good about that season? Is it time for any

of it to die?
3. Where and how were you relationally connected? Whom do you miss? What do you miss about him or her?
4. How were you spiritually fed in that season?
5. What is God inviting you to do more of or to try in this season?
6. What is hard for you in this season?

In this liminal space where your old life is gone, savor the empty spring field of this year. In Matthew 13:3 Jesus said, "A farmer went out to sow his seed." You know what happened: some fell on the path, some on the rocks, and some amongst the thorns. "Still other seed fell on good soil, where it produced a crop—a hundred, sixty or thirty times what was sown. Whoever has ears, let them hear" (Matthew 13:8–9). Though Jesus is talking about people hearing the gospel, you too can hear good news Jesus has just for you and still live your life in such a way that you end up burnt out, discouraged, and isolated on the field. Jesus calls you to tend your soul in such a way where you are like the good soil, ready to receive the seeds that Jesus wants to plant. The good news is for you too.

The Responsibility
While this season is a gift, it also comes with responsibilities. You know from this chapter that you will need to be more involved and proactive in your spiritual feeding than at other times. On the one hand, this has become easier as more options are available today in the form of books, podcasts,

sermons, even live streaming of events—all good choices. But also find ways for God Himself to feed you directly that do not rely on internet connections or time zone converting.

"As long as I kept moving, my grief streamed out behind me like a swimmer's long hair in water. I knew the weight was there but it didn't touch me. Only when I stopped did the slick, dark stuff of it come float in around my face, catching my arms and throat till I began to drown. So I just didn't stop."[21] (Emphasis mine.) These words, from Barbara Kingsolver's *The Poisonwood Bible*, are spoken by Orleanna after the death of her youngest, Ruth May. You are probably from a culture where moving nonstop is valued. And the energy required to get you to the field? I bet you could fill notebooks with the stories. The mantra of *just keep moving, no matter what* served you well to get you here. But what got you here might end up killing you.

You probably know that slowing down, even stopping, is God's best for you. So this message is no surprise. But it is risky because when you slow down, you don't know what will catch up. Orleanna knew that it was her grief she was trying to stay ahead of. You might be trying to outrun insecurity, disappointment, betrayal, or fear that you won't be provided for. No matter what you are trying to keep at bay, even if subconsciously, God is bigger than it and God does not want you beholden to it. When you slow down, God may want to assure you that you are enough, that you are a good parent, that your efforts at studying the language are admirable, or

---

21 Barbara Kingsolver, *The Poisonwood Bible* (New York: HarperCollins, 1998), 381.

that He will take care of a burden you are carrying. But slowing down is often easier said than done. So the first way to allow God to feed you is to slow down with a daily practice of solitude, silence, and stillness.

If you are like me, these practices will feel a bit ridiculous at first. And unnatural and eternal. I can produce like a workhorse. If you need something done, I am your person. But withdraw and sit alone for five minutes? Agony. Be quiet without any background noise or multitasking? (Isn't that why God made podcasts?) Boring. Stop moving without reading or scrolling through my phone? I start jonesing like the distraction addict I am.

On the field many of you find yourselves in environments that have more noise, more people, crowded public transportation, cramped living situations, slower internet, busy open markets, and almost-constant crisis. Noise. Movement. Distraction. It would help if you had three-day rotation of daily rhythms involving solitude, silence, and stillness. In brief, here are descriptions of these three practices:

Solitude. "Even when we aren't physically present with each other, our days are punctuated with texts, tweets, and social media interactions. But somehow people still feel deeply and profoundly lonely. Solitude, intentional withdrawal, teaches us to be present—present to ourselves, present to God, and present with others."[22] If you are wired to help people, get a rush from being needed, or find your worth in

---

22 Christopher L. Heuertz, *The Sacred Enneagram: Finding Your Unique Path to Spiritual Growth* (Grand Rapids, MI: Zondervan, 2017), 171.

GOD AND YOU

solving problems, solitude will be a challenge for you. But as you start with five minutes alone with God—not checking your phone, not listening to a sermon, not doing anything that might be deemed helpful to others—you will grow in your ability to be present with your family, your team, and the locals you have come to serve.

Silence. Escaping noise is virtually impossible without intention. Traffic, music, sports, entertainment, children, construction, even household appliances add to the cacophony. Gordon Hempton is an acoustic ecologist and collects sound all over the world. He says that quiet is a "think tank of the soul."[23] Enter the practice of silence. "Silence actually teaches us to listen. It helps us learn how to listen to the voice of God, a voice we maybe have not been able to recognize. It helps us listen to the people in our lives who speak loving, truthful words of correction or affirmation to us. In silence we hear the truth that God is not as hard on us as we are on ourselves."[24]

Stillness. Technology has changed how I consume information; too often my ability to focus resembles a pinball machine. While I am tempted to blame the "reality of modern life," the truth is I have let many of these distractions into my life believing that their benefits outweigh their costs. The practice of stillness completes the three-day rotation. "In addition to our drive to build a better world, we also live in a time when productivity and impact feed the lies we believe

---

[23] Krista Tippet, *"Gordon Hempton: Silence and the Presence of Everything,"* On Being, May 10, 2012 updated December 29, 2016, https://onbeing.org/programs/gordon-hempton-silence-and-the-presence-of-everything.

[24] Heuertz, *The Sacred Enneagram*, 171

GETTING STARTED

about ourselves. The constant pressure to do more, to fill up our schedules, to work harder. Stillness teaches us restraint, and in restraint we are able to discern what appropriate engagement looks like."[25] Sit. Lie on your bed. Find a rock, a bench, a small corner of nature, and do not move. Be still for five minutes. Like Orleanna, see what catches up with you.

God will feed you through sermons, books (my personal favorite), podcasts (a close second for me), and worship music. But God will also nourish your straight from Himself. Start with five minutes of solitude on day one, five minutes of silence on day two, and five minutes of stillness on day three. Over time, begin to add on, until you have fifteen minutes of sustained solitude, silence, or stillness. Instead of trying to run ahead of the loneliness, loss, and longing you will experience this year, allow these practices to root you more firmly in God. Your ability to be present, to listen, and to engage with those around you will increase as you hear from Him.

The Promise

Panel one of the tryptic contains the gift of this year and a chance to reflect on your life and put in place habits and rhythms that will spiritually feed you. The middle panel holds the responsibility that you will need to participate in your spiritual feeding more than you did back home. In the final panel is the promise that God *will* feed you as He meets you, stretches you, comforts you, and goes before you. That does

---

25 Ibid., 171.

not mean that you are guaranteed a "good" year, or a deep understanding of what God is doing, or even the sense of His presence. As the writer of Ecclesiastes says, "This, too, I carefully explored: Even though the actions of godly and wise people are in God's hands, no one knows whether God will show them favor" (Ecclesiastes 9:1 NLT). My hope and prayer is that you have deep communion with God this year, but if you do not, you can trust in the promise that you have not been abandoned.

Before we end this chapter, here are a few of the insights people shared in the survey when it came to their relationships with God during the first year:

"Calm down, relax. Your fears are unfounded (well, most of them), you'll be able to communicate soon, so relax and trust the process, and most of all, don't set aside your time with God for the more urgent tasks of your day."

"Journal and keep the daily discipline of Bible reading (even if short) as a sacred duty; that it is how God speaks to you. Do not depend on others for soul nourishment. You are not too busy! Read a Psalm a day and ask God to speak to you. Psalms are mental health food and medicine; their beauty transports you to where your soul needs to be. They teach you how to express your emotions (a huge part of the first year) and mold your emotions as God works through them. When you finish Psalms, start over. You will never regret this."

"God is already there and at work. He didn't come with you. Look for where He is already at work. Your job is to know

Him and to be faithful in all He calls you to. It's not all up to you. Work hard, but also spend time with the landlord and neighbor, not to achieve your goal of language learning but to get to know them. Loving God and loving people only comes from knowing God and knowing people. Ask God to do these things within you, for it is from Him and not your own effort that it can be done."

"My theology was all messed up, thinking that if I followed God's leading, I would surely have joy. Instead, I ended up depressed. When my support systems were taken away, I was not as resilient as I thought I was."

Plastic Chopsticks Are the Worst

Just as you are physically learning to feed yourself, you are also spiritually learning to feed yourself in new ways. I grew to hate using plastic chopsticks when I was eating with students or school officials. Without fail, food slipped out—and a few embarrassing times I actually shot food across the table. I longed for bamboo chopsticks because food stuck to them better and they felt a tad more familiar. As you learn to eat with your hands, chopsticks, or the knife in your left (or right) hand, God is also teaching you new ways to nourish yourself spiritually. And who knows, the day may come when church back home becomes the strange way to "do church" or be fed. Regardless, here is a truth: God never tires of feeding His children.

7
New Relationships (But Not with People)

Of all the changes I experienced moving to the field, the change in my relationship with finances was the most obvious to me. Pre-field I taught in a public school for several years and earned a "real" salary. Moving from a "real" job to a "ministry" one meant that my finances went from being (mostly) my business to the whole wide world's business. Not quite, but that is how it felt. I needed to add my parents to my bank accounts so they could handle financial stuff in the States; I needed to discuss specific dollar needs and funds raised with anyone who would listen, and I needed to decide whether or not I wanted to raise more money to cover "nonessentials." (I did not, a decision I would come to regret when I did not have medical evacuation insurance.) As a teacher I knew I earned my salary through my hard work. As a cross-cultural worker I did not make money; I raised support and lived off the generosity and faithfulness of many dear people. To this day, decades later, I still find myself thinking in terms of earning a "real" salary versus being on full-time support. But money was not the only area I needed to redefine and relearn as a cross-cultural worker.

When you move overseas, you take all of yourself. So, in addition to your suitcases, you will also bring along concepts about finances, your body, the weather, success and productivity, social media, and time. While you might not encounter significant changes in all of these areas this year, you may over time. Part of this first year is about tearing down ideas and allowing God to usher in a new way of relating to each. While I have not read this book, I love the title: *What Got You Here Won't Get You There*.[26] In other words, what helped you in your home country may not help you in your new country when it comes to finances, your body, the weather, success and productivity, social media, and time. Changing your relationships with some of these areas will be easier than it is with others. Some will feel like a wrestling match with God and leave you with a limp. All will influence you this year.

Real versus Ministry

The amount of money I needed to raise my first year did not seem astronomical, and I planned to be on the field for two years and return to my "real" life. So I sent out letters, met with people, tracked financial and prayer commitments, and was blessed to be fully funded when I left for the field. My feelings toward money were mild that first year. If you think you will be on the field for a specific time period, say one to four years, you will still experience changes in your thoughts and beliefs about money. Even if mental math isn't your strength, conversion rates may make a mathematician

---

26 Marshall Goldsmith, *What Got You Here Won't Get You There*, (New York: Hyperion, 2007).

NEW RELATIONSHIPS (BUT NOT WITH PEOPLE)

of you yet. The first few years I lived in China, the conversion rate was 8.3 yuan to one US dollar. I was grateful that, for the most part, I could divide by eight and didn't have to convert a currency that was in the thousands or millions compared to US dollars.

When it came time for my dad to do my taxes in America, reality began to sink in. My annual income dropped by 87.5 percent; said another way, my yearly income dropped by thousands of dollars and all I could do was laugh. On the surface, my life looked similar enough. In both America and China, I had a home, was well (enough) dressed, had access to medical care (even though the level was different), had enough food, running water, and electricity to live a comfortable life, and was able to travel. Why did an 87.5 percent decrease stand out to me when it had not radically changed the quality of my physical life?

And now we are back to the idea of a "real" salary. As I worked on this chapter, it struck me that we only use the word "real" with "salary." When was the last time you heard the phrase "my real body" as opposed to a "my ministry body"? You don't. You have a body, I have a body. Or "real weather" versus "ministry weather"? No such distinction. The enemy may have also warped the idea of "real" when it comes to your livelihood.

As your relationship with money changes, you will experience a transformation in three areas: privacy, provision, and pleasure.

GETTING STARTED

Privacy

In the West, money is relegated to the "private" part of a person's life. Because it is private, we don't tend to know how to talk about finances, which can lead to isolation and ignorance on how to handle money. When it comes to cross-cultural workers, this discussion of money is complicated because three parties are involved: the individual or family, the sending organization, and the supporters. While many financial decisions will still be your personal business, you will have more people aware of your finances than you did pre-field. Boundaries with money will continue to be appropriate, though God may move those boundaries and what you consider to be "your private business" may need to flex.

Provision

One of the myths about provision is that men have a harder time being on support than women do, and this myth is cited as one of the reasons more women are on the field than men. In my humble opinion, this is nonsense. Raising support lays bare the illusion that you are providing for yourself—which is beautiful and hard. God has probably already amazed you in the ways He has moved people to support you. One of the hymns I wanted to sing every Sunday my first year was *Great Is Your Faithfulness* because it verbalized the bursting feelings in my heart. But money is still complex because identity is tied to money for many of us. This year, keep exploring your beliefs and values as you see resistance, discomfort, joy, and security within you. Pray for God's provision, be faithful in doing your part to communicate with supporters, and record how God meets your financial needs.

Pleasure

One of the big questions related to being on support is, "Can you have fun on supporters' money?"—with subquestions related to vacations, dessert, even buying a quality mattress when you could make do with a cheaper one. The short answer is yes, you can. But this year you will begin to wrestle with where lines should be drawn for you and your family. These conversations will continue to unfold over the years. You are called to live by faith and believe in a loving God who provides. Money is not to be your idol, source of security, or source of identity; and it can be a conduit of fun, blessing, and memory making.

Questioning Your Beef Consumption
In my journal I wrote, "Lunch with students Zhu Hui (female) and Li Fei (male) was nice. Li Fei wondered if the tires on my bike were oval because both Erin and I had been riding on it. He said, 'I know in your country you're average, but here you are . . . giants!' Thanks for spelling that out, Li Fei. Sigh." It was true: compared to my students I was a giant. I often had to remind myself that my students were adults, even though they were similar in size to my American junior higher students. I was asked if I ate too much beef as a child and was informed that Americans are fat because "they all like to eat cheese and butter." This line was repeated so often I eventually learned it was from a nationally used high school

English textbook.

The comments, oh, the comments. Not to set you up to be defensive from the get-go, but as a gentle warning, the proverbial wisdom to *guard your heart* is also meant for your first year on the field. I came to see the sense in the cliché that *ignorance is bliss* after I learned the Chinese word for "fat" and realized how many people were saying, "That foreigner is fat." It was a small mercy I did not learn in the first year to say, "I am neither a giant, nor fat, nor a consumer of copious amounts of beef, nor a cheese-loving butter eater, you tiny little rude runt!"

Even if you are similarly sized to the people you have come to serve, you will experience a new relationship with your body and your health. I lived in the land of spicy food, and my teammate and I had the code phrase "hot-pot butt" for the additional bathroom time required after especially spicy meals. At times it felt like my intestines were being squeezed out of me. You will discuss your body and its function in ways that might make your pre-field self blush. Beyond food, you and your body might experience repeated malaria, insomnia, panic attacks, or endless stomach bugs.

The subject of the body and health came up in the survey as well:

"I loved finally being on the field after a long buildup, I connected well with host friends, and I felt fulfilled. But I also suffered from the worst insomnia ever (couple hours a night for nine months); I had to deal with inappropriate physical touch from a local coworker; I wished I could learn the language quicker, and adjustment to team culture was hard."

NEW RELATIONSHIPS (BUT NOT WITH PEOPLE)

"The advice I give to people new to the field is don't be afraid to nap when you need it."

"I was constantly anxious due to parts of my job and often had insomnia."

"We unexpectedly relocated after our first four weeks, which became a good thing but was challenging. I broke my foot after a month or so of being in the new location, and there was little medical care. We could not even get it X-rayed and were on the fourth floor with only stairs."

"We had a series of health crises, including a medivac for our youngest son (who was two years old at the time), and two times where he was close to death. We ended up on furlough three years later with both my husband and I being burnt out and we were not doing well in our marriage."

"It was one of the hardest years ever. By the end of first year I had stomach ulcers and was questioning if I had even heard God at all."

You are fearfully and wonderfully made, but you are not without limits. Be kind to your body, and help your children be kind to theirs. Your digestive system is adjusting to new food, water, and bugs. Your nervous system is adjusting to new stimuli. Your respiratory system is adjusting to different air, flowers, and pollution. Try to rest more than you did in your home country. Even if you are raring to go, establish a rhythm that has both raring and resting. And if someone asks you if you ate too much beef as a child, ask God to help you maintain your sense of humor and keep you tender toward those you came to serve.

Because, honestly, it is funny. Save that story for a newsletter!

Is That Celsius or Fahrenheit?
I heard that Chengdu was humid but did not think much of it because I had been living in Lawrence, Kansas, a humid city compared to the arid Colorado climate I grew up in. Before moving to Chengdu, I spent two humidity-dripping summers in China and had lived to tell the tale. I thought I would be fine. Early on, my journal mentions the weather, but the tone began to change in November. "Monday's composition test went well, and the students thought it was brilliant to read their roommate descriptions out loud. The only downside was that my feet were so cold I wanted to die!" Later in the evening of the same day, Erin and I gave a culture lecture, and when we got home, I "graded a little and then bathed. Bathing is both wonderful and terrible because we have hot water, but when it is time to dry off, I am miserably cold."

Between the idea that fresh air is good for your health (windows were always open) and the fact that the government did not provide heating for the southern half of the country, I was only warm in bed. I was from Colorado, for Pete's sake; how could I be this cold? Erin and I learned to dress in layers and hold cups of hot water to keep warm. No matter how many layers I put on to teach—and I was able to squeeze into three layers on the bottom, seven on top, and two pairs of socks—I often could not feel my feet when I walked home because they were so cold.

Some of my students' hands swelled and turned red. Others experienced cracks along the ridges of their ears, and eventually the open sores would scab over. When students visited our home, they often apologized for wiggling, saying that their feet were so uncomfortable in our "warm" apartment (we had the windows closed) and the heat made their feet swell and itch. When I gently asked students why their hands were swollen, their ears scabbed, or their feet itchy, they looked up the word *chilblains* in their dictionary. I vaguely recalled hearing *chilblains* abound in classic books like *Jane Eyre* but did not know they existed in modern day. My students explained that if you got too cold as a child, the nerve damage was permanent and every winter when the weather changed, they suffered.

I was not the only one to experience a new relationship with the weather. In the survey, people mentioned it too:

"The winter weather ended up being the hardest part. I thought I was going to freeze to death during my first few months in Portugal. No heat, tile floors."

"Moving to Tanzania was a very hard year for all the usual culture shock moments. Holidays were now HOT instead of cold. They were without family. It was just a really hard transition."

"The constant heat and humidity were so oppressive."

"I gave my year a three out of ten because my bad days kind

of outweighed the good. We had our first baby three months after arriving. My husband grew up as an MK, so I was often compared to him and felt pressured by him (unintentionally) to stay caught up. I jumped in with both feet and kind of drowned. Language seemed to elude me. Still does. Add hundred-degree weather and a baby who doesn't sleep well at night, and I went into a bit of a depression."

"My year was a 'three' because we were dropped off without any real orientation to our new city, no one to teach us where or how to shop or cook. Our assigned ministry was made unavailable. Heat, mosquitoes, noise, and a surprise pregnancy knocked the rest of the wind out of our sails."

For moms, the weather can be challenging because it is so cold (or hot) that their kids cannot play outside. Finding ways to occupy a child in meaningful ways inside for days, weeks, even months is hard. If you find yourself in this position and are discouraged, be gracious with yourself. Mild depression can be a normal reaction to being cooped up.

The Chengdu winters changed me, and I still do not like to be cold because I am afraid that I am going to be frozen for months. In your first year, if you are in a cold place as well, one day you will see people beating the dead leaves out of the trees with brooms and realize spring has arrived. You have lived through your first winter, and just as you learn new signs of the changing seasons, you will realize you are changing too.

That Was a Good Day

I didn't read *Tattoos on the Heart* by Father Gregory Boyle before my first year on the field. But I so wish I had. Father Gregory's chapter on "Success" verbalized what I want you to know this first year. "People want me to tell them success stories. I understand this. They are the stories you want to tell, after all. So why does my scalp tighten whenever I am asked this? Surely, part of it comes from my being utterly convinced I'm a fraud. Twenty years of this work has taught me that God has greater comfort with inverting categories than I do. What is success and what is failure? What is good and what is bad? Setback or progress?"[27]

God has greater comfort with inverting categories than I do. Same here, Father Gregory, same here. This year your ideas of success will need to be examined. In general, for me success looks like getting this book done. I love to accomplish tasks. For instance, I had hoped to have this book completed before an upcoming trip to Indonesia, but seeing as I leave in roughly sixty hours and still have several chapters to write . . . ain't gonna happen. Even during this "important ministry project," I am invited (again) by God to look at how I define success and invited (again) by God to redefine it. In this case, I am redefining success as finishing this chapter before I board the plane. But in some cases success is not easy to redefine. If you work with orphans, is success when a child is placed in a stable home? If you work in the medical field, is success helping people die with dignity? If you are in translation

---

[27] Gregory Boyle, *Tattoos on the Heart: The Power of Boundless Compassion* (New York: Free Press, 2010), 167.

GETTING STARTED

work, is it only the finished Bible?

This section is not one to rush through. Take time to think about the questions below, and find someone to discuss your thoughts to success.

- What will success look like this year?
- What will success in daily life, ministry life, team life, and personal life look like?
- In which area are you most susceptible to be hard on yourself and feel like a failure?
- What is God trying to show you about Himself and about yourself this year?

Father Gregory reminds us that "the tyranny of success often can't be bothered with complexity."[28] Welcome to complexity. I mean that in all sincerity. God is going to grow and challenge and encourage and confuse you this year. Part of being a success is paying attention to the ways God is at work in you as well as in those you have come to serve. Father Gregory quoted Mary Oliver who said, "There are things you can't reach. But you can reach out to them, all day long."[29] This year you will reach toward a new idea of success.

Related to success is the idea of productivity. At the end of many a day, I was struck by the sense of "What did I do today?!" because a day might have been filled with doing laundry, going to the post office, and having lunch with a student. Really? Why did it take so much time to do so little?

---

28 Ibid., 169.
29 Ibid., 186.

NEW RELATIONSHIPS (BUT NOT WITH PEOPLE)

My sense of a "productive" day had to change, or I would be the busiest, most unproductive human on the planet. Add to the mix the fact that Erin and I were both new to the area, so we had to figure life out on our own without a veteran to show us the ropes, and it meant that we scored high on the buddy system and low on the efficiency scale. When asked in the survey what ended up being the hardest part of the first year, this sense of how much time goes to mere survival or maintaining a household repeatedly came up:

"Just household and survival stuff like learning to travel with taxis in a difficult urban poor environment, no good carryout options, so food had to be well planned and took more time and of course lots of traveler's tummy issues."

"Survival ended up being the hardest. Eating, staying healthy, finances, I mean very basic stuff."

"Cooking and doing food ended up taking so much time!"

"The difficulty of finding and cooking food without refrigeration or car."

"The first few weeks figuring out how to get food while feeling lost and overwhelmed."

What stands out to me is how much these responses mirror the reality: short sentences holding hours of activity. When Father Gregory talked about God inverting categories, he could have included productivity as well. As I read through my journal, I see that my days were full. The rub—even now when I reflect on those days—is that the amount of time specific tasks took felt inordinately out of proportion to what they "should" have taken. When I reflect on a day, a week, a month, and I evaluate it on how many new words I learned, how much time was spent waiting in line for my paperwork, or how much time was spent walking from place to place, it is tempting to view life as having clear goals that can be evaluated. That which can be measured can be improved, I falsely believed.

What if God wants to invert your idea of productivity? The *more* He is interested in is His *presence*, not what you get done. Instead of accomplishing more, I encourage you to see success as being fully present in whatever your day holds. Yes, you need to get things done for your job, your ministry, and your daily life. I am not advocating a kumbaya approach or suggesting you should not be frustrated with systems that are broken. But if you do not change the way you relate to and think about productivity this year, you risk feeling that you are not accomplishing what you should be, when in reality your calling invariably involves presence more than production.

Done In by A Pumpkin Latte

You live in a marvelous time when travel and communication are becoming easier and easier. You also live in a time when the abundance of technology and social media invites you to be present in two worlds. Some agencies have policies to help their people bond to the people and work in their new location. Whether you have an organization that restricts you having visitors, traveling back home, or dating during your first year, you will still have choices.

NEW RELATIONSHIPS (BUT NOT WITH PEOPLE)

I am going to sound like I am about five thousand years old. But it was not that long ago I took pictures of my life with friends and family, had them developed, and mailed the photos back to the United States. Now, you carry a small computer in your pockets and have options on how to share your life. Friends and family can be more invested in your life than in any time in history. They can pray for you in real time. They can actually see a meal or an event as it is happening. They can walk with you to the market. Children can see distant relatives on video chats.

Not only can you share your life, but in real time you can watch friends' lives in photos, updates, and video clips. You can see how your sports team did without waiting for an expensive call or newspaper clippings . . . and possibly even watch a game live, even in the middle of the night. You can pray for your mom on FaceTime before she goes into surgery and hear the doctor's post-surgery report with your siblings. All of these are blessings upon blessings.

But what if you are not bonding because your teammate is, and you say this with all the love of Jesus, an idiot? It's reasonable that you would rather connect with your friends back home. What if it is so hot outside you cannot bear to go to the market? Instead, you stay in your air-conditioned apartment, watching a show online, and remind yourself that no one died from eating crackers five days in a row. What if your child will not interact with your neighbors and only wants to play video games? What if seeing the seasonal beverages on social media fosters jealousy?

This year your relationship with technology needs to be one of discernment and noticing the posture of your heart and soul. Discernment is knowing when to adjust for a season. If seeing pumpkin lattes is not good for your heart, maybe take a break for a few days. If you typically love to cheer for your team, yet find that you are inordinately focused on their standing, experiment with limits.

God is for you. He also may love the cooking show you love, the sports team you follow, and surely your friend who is getting married. He is also as interested in what is forming and informing you. Here is a simple litmus test for the year: When you get off the phone or have spent an hour on social media, do you feel connected or disconnected from God, yourself, or your life? Though written almost two thousand years ago, Paul's words are as timely for you as they were for the Galatians (read Galatians 5:19–25 to see what I mean). In general, does your use of technology result in the fruit of the Spirit? Responding with the fruit of the Spirit does not mean you are always happy, but that you have patience or kindness. Instead, do you feel stirred up, numb, increasingly jealous when you get offline? Paul calls these signs of the flesh. Signs of the fruit of the flesh include hatred, discord, jealousy, fits of rage, selfish ambition, dissensions, factions or envy. A quick check of your head, heart, and gut will let you spot these signs.

You can have an off day, but if you observe that "every time" you are on social media, you are discontent with your apartment or so sad you cannot be at your nephew's games, talk to God about His best for you. As you navigate your evolving relationship with technology living at a distance from friends and family, imagine you are on a road with changing speed limits. What is a safe speed in one part of the journey may put you in great danger in another part.

NEW RELATIONSHIPS (BUT NOT WITH PEOPLE)

Making a Masterpiece

Your first year on the field can feel like you are in a bizarre time warp. As I mentioned above, daily tasks for me took an excessive amount of time. But once life was up and running, paradoxically I had more time on my hands than I wanted. Over the months, as I got to know people, my schedule filled up, but for the first few months Erin and I played endless games of Yahtzee (her choice) and Skip-Bo (my choice). Playing Skip-Bo at 7:15 a.m. after breakfast, killing time until we left for our 8:00 a.m. classes, did not fit with the mental picture I had had of myself as a cross-cultural worker. I certainly was not writing home about how often Erin and I played games because we were bored.

China had the habit of a *xiu-xi*, or rest time, from noon-ish to 2:00 p.m. Coming from a culture that viewed napping as something only the young, the old, and the sick did, at first I found having a large chunk of time dead in the middle of the day maddening. While I loved the relative peace and quiet, I was frustrated I could not run any of the errands on my to-do lists because everyone was xiu-xi-ing. Over time, I grew to love having a quiet period to read or work on grading. Erin and I would spend time praying after lunch, knowing that we were less likely to be interrupted. God used the cultural difference to begin to rewire me.

Your new culture may not have a siesta time, but the norms surrounding time will vary from your passport culture. How long will a meal take? Who initiates ending a meal? What is considered being early, on time, or late? How long is a church service, a visit to a sick friend, or a conversation with a neighbor? I knew the answers to these questions when I was in America, but I had to learn them in China. A fun part of moving to a new culture is learning a new way of life. A maddening part of moving to a new culture is learning a new way of life.

This year, as you establish new norms—both from the culture and from the opportunity new beginnings offer—consider how white space can be used by God in the tending of your soul, your family, and your work. "In graphic design, whitespace is a key element to the aesthetic quality of composition. The more fine art a composition is, the more whitespace you'll find. The more commercial the piece, the more text and images you'll find crowded in. The purpose is no longer beauty. *It is commercialization.* Whitespace keeps the message from being cluttered and draws attention to what is important. *Is my faith more like art or cluttered advertisement?*"[30]

As new norms and rhythms are lived into this year, what a powerful question to ask when it comes to time: *Are my faith and life more like art or cluttered advertisement?*

God is a relational God. Too often the word "relationship" is limited to people. As image bearers, human relationships are primary, yet they are not the only ones we have. Your person-to-person relationships are influenced by your relationships with finances, your body, the weather, success and productivity, social media, and time. This year, intentionally create space for these relationships to be informed and formed by your new culture and your role in the Great Commission.

---

30 Bonnie Gray, *Finding Spiritual Whitespace: Awakening Your Soul to Rest* (Grand Rapids: Revell, 2014), 67–68.

8
Four Languages You Didn't Know You'd Learn

I fear that as you read this chapter, you will feel like I am dog-piling on you, or worse, God is. Moving to China, I knew I would need to learn about Chinese culture and language. I knew not only that I would need to learn, I was eager to. Well, let me clarify. I was keen to learn about Chinese culture and assumed that I would stink at learning Chinese. Three years of studying German in high school left me with the ability to say my name and that I lived in a "one-family dwelling house"—a line from a dialogue seared into my memory. In college I planned to become a high school Russian language teacher. What a colossal disaster that turned out to be. Looking back, I can see that I was pretty much set up to fail at learning Russian, but I did not know it at the time. My takeaway was that I was terrible at learning languages and good at learning math, so I should stick to my lane. I was certainly open to learning Chinese, but not hopeful.

Good golly, I had no idea that Chinese language and culture were the tip of the iceberg of what I would learn. Several themes came up in the survey pointing to sublanguages cross-cultural workers need to be versed in, in addition

GETTING STARTED

to the language of the people they have come to serve. This is where I do not want you to feel overwhelmed at all that you will need to assimilate. While it's true you will need to learn to speak all of these sublanguages, think of this chapter as more an introduction to them, instead of a warning that you'd better be fluent in them or else! Picture us chatting over a Thai iced tea. We are not in a classroom, and you are not wildly taking notes, hoping you remember everything so that you can pass the test.

Like any other language, the goal is fluency, not perfection. Words can be tricky, and nuanced, and loaded. Over time you will learn the grammar of grief, the syntax of celebration, the tenses of stress, and the parsing of suffering.

The Grammar of Grief

I laughed when I read a recent email I received.[31] I met Jill several years ago when she was a college intern for a Christian nonprofit I work with. She is now in full-time ministry in Los Angeles after a few years of living in India. I had hit reply to her newsletter and written that I loved how we are both in Kingdom work.

She replied, "We recently had an all-day training on the 'first term' overseas. The facilitator emphasized the importance of grieving . . . I had a flashback to the summer internship when you were discussing grieving with the interns. We were talking about our grieving process, and when it got to me to share, I said, 'I don't think I grieve.' You looked me straight in the face and, in the most Amy-Young-type way,

---

31 Name changed, email message to author, March 4, 2019.

said (very lovingly obviously), 'Well, that's not healthy.' Ha-ha! That was the start of my grieving journey and learning how to grieve. It was an invaluable lesson to for life overseas."

If you have read *Looming Transitions*, you know that grief is discussed throughout the book and highlighted in two chapters. Part of what you need to know about yourself is your grieving style. Are you a pre-griever, doing the majority of your grieving before an event? Or are you a post-griever and grieve primarily after an event? Regardless of your grieving style, grief is a part of the cross-cultural life. You will miss times with family "back home," you will be exposed to injustices that leave you feeling helpless, and your calling will cost you personally. Learning to speak grief is a three-fold process: tune in, name it, and grieve it.

Grief often does not come to your front door and announce herself like a formal guest. Instead, she will sneak around to the side window and enter like a thief. She will cozy up to the fireplace of your heart and blow on the embers of annoyance and irritation because they are more empowering to feel than sadness and loss. By tuning in to your hurt, your annoyance, your emotional distance, your anger, and your constant need to stay busy, you might notice that sometimes they are disguises for grief.

Once you have tuned in to what is going on, name it. Let grief know she does not (always) have to play games to get your attention. No matter how fluently you speak grief, sometimes she still will enter through the back door, and that is just how it is. Whether grief comes in through the front door or not, once you know it is in your house, name it. Say something like, "Hello, grief. I hate that you are here.

I hate that I need to grieve my kids not being around their grandparents for the trillionth time today. But I see you, and I'm saying hello."

And then grieve. "Because you'll die a thousand mini-deaths, there will not be one way to grieve. Instead in the messy middle there are as many ways to grieve as there are things to be grieved!"[32] You can get more ideas on how to grieve from *Looming Transitions*. As one survey participant told her first-year self, "You are grieving everything you left behind, and yes, this year sucks. Just own it. It won't break you; in fact, it will become a powerful part of your story. God hasn't abandoned you; He is just reworking you and preparing you for fruitful ministry in the coming years."

While transitions are an easier time to identify what you will lose, they are a terrible time to begin practicing the language of grief. If you can start to speak this sublanguage now, your time will be enhanced because grief is a two-for-one. You cannot turn down the volume on the painful emotions without also turning down the internal volume on the positive ones.[33] So, one of the best ways to practice joy is to learn her sister language, grief.

The Syntax of Celebration

I have a mixed relationship with Hudson Taylor. If you are not familiar with him, Hudson Taylor is the founder of the

---

32 Amy Young, *Looming Transitions*, 126.
33 Brené Brown, *The Gifts of Imperfection: Let Go of Who You Think You're Supposed to Be and Embrace Who You Are* (Center City, MN.: Hazelden, 2010), 72.

China Inland Mission. Every location around the world will have a "famous" cross-cultural servant, and since I lived in China, Hudson Taylor is mine. Phrases used to describe him in a well-known biography include that he "experienced difficulties such as few have ever encountered, led tens of thousands of souls to eternal life, mobilized 1,200 workers, and never mentioned financial appeals yet was never in debt."[34] I understand why Hudson Taylor's life is biography worthy, but the problem for most of us common folks is that these "famous" stories warp our sense of what is to be celebrated. One of the saddest truths about cross-cultural workers is that as a whole we are so focused on the *big picture*, we forget the importance of the *small ordinary*.

This year, if you do not begin to speak the language of celebration over your life and work, you may feed the lie that much of your life is not enough. As one survey participant wrote, "Celebrate the small victories, they add up to something of eternal value! Spend the first year coming in as a learner. Don't expect any movement or progress on your own agenda. Take time to see how and why things are already done before you go in and change things. Ask questions. Never stop asking questions." The posture of a learner is critical, but also consider and remember: what do learners do? They learn, often through trial and error.

It is no small feat to enter a new culture, a new way of ministering, and get a life up and running . . . with minimal language skills possibly for weeks or months. (Or years. I'm

---

[34] Howard Taylor and Geraldine Taylor, *Hudson Taylor's Spiritual Secret*, (Chicago: Moody, 2009), 16.

GETTING STARTED

looking at you, Amy.) But you probably are not giving yourself enough credit for how hard it is. Cultural mistakes stick in your brain like they're attached with Velcro, while cultural achievements slide off like an egg in a Teflon pan.

Richard Rohr explains the Velcro and Teflon reaction of your brain this way. "Negativity, fear, resentment, and anger attach like Velcro and imprint readily. They are addictive. It's a strange attractor. While positivity—joy, gratitude, etc.—is like Teflon, and slides off readily. It takes a minimum of 15 seconds of savoring for the brain to hold it and imprint the positive experience."[35]

By savoring a part of your life for fifteen seconds, you are practicing the language of celebration. One way to savor and create Velcro hooks for the positive is to record small events. I wrote in my journal, "Erin and I stopped at a small store to buy a bag of White Rabbit candy for ¥6.5 from the nicest man. I gave him a ¥10 and he held out a ¥5 and wanted more money. It took me a while to understand that he didn't have small change and wanted ¥11.50 so that he could give me a ¥5 in change. We decided to stop for *jiaozi*. I went next door to buy water since Chinese don't normally drink while eating. I am so proud of myself for being able to ask how much things cost and then actually buy them! After lunch—which was delicious and we got to sit under the ceiling fan—we bought Pepsi and made photocopies. We

---

[35] Richard Rohr, "Gleaning From Richard Rohr," *Urban Suburban Clergy Group*, April 2016, http://www.saintmarks.org/wp-content/uploads/2015/09/Gleanings-from-Richard-Rohr-April-2016-SMC-Thomason.pdf

came home quite pleased with all we had accomplished."

Speaking the language of celebration begins to train you to see God at work in the day-to-day, not waiting "until." It also trains you to value the small, easy-to-overlook parts of life on the road to the so-called real action. God included small examples in the Bible:

- the mustard seed (Matthew 13:31–32)
- the approval of the widow who gave her last two coins (Mark 12:41–44)
- the little boy's paltry lunch (John 6:9)
- a small coin in a fish's mouth to pay taxes (Matthew 17:27)
- the tax collector in a sycamore tree (Luke 19:1–10)
- two sparrows sold for a penny yet not one of them will fall to the ground outside of God's care (Matthew 10:29–31)
- God numbered the hairs on your head (Luke 12:7).

You can hear the joy in the following survey response: "My first solo taxi ride, though it sounds small, it was a HUGE victory for me. I was able to give enough directions (in Arabic) to get me close to my final destination without getting us completely lost. It was a victory in language as well as for this directionally challenged gal!" This person has learned to speak the language of celebration.

The Tenses of Stress

Our school was located on a major road that cut through the middle of Chengdu. The campus was surrounded by a brick wall that had shards of broken glass sticking out of the top of the wall. The front gate was manned 24/7 by a guard who monitored the comings and goings of everyone on campus. On either side of the front gate were two tall dormitories, one for the men and the other for the women. Since we were teaching adults, outside of the classroom our students were more like friends. One afternoon my first year, Erin and I bumped into several of our students near the front gate. Somehow the conversation turned to the walls that surrounded the campus. That explosion you hear? It was my mind being blown.

"Wait," I said, trying to let the reality of what Wen Bing said catch up with me yet not let shock show on my face. "So, you *like* the walls? You like having a guard? You don't mind that someone monitors your coming and going? Or that the gate is locked at 10:00 p.m. and you need to be inside before it is locked? You don't find the walls confining?"

I did not actually say all of this, but I sure thought it. I was not the only one with my mind blown. Wen Bing and his classmate almost had to lift their jaws from the dusty ground. "Wait, you *aren't* proud of the walls? And the way they represent that our school takes safety so seriously? You don't find them comforting? Your American universities do *not* have walls and you still feel safe? You hate the walls?"

A few weeks earlier Erin and I had a similar "wall" conversation, but the subject was chains. As you know, we lived in a guesthouse—think small, not-well-maintained hotel—on our campus. Every evening when the campus gates were locked, the front door of the guesthouse was locked by a long bicycle chain, which wrapped around the door handles and clicked

FOUR LANGUAGES YOU DIDN'T KNOW YOU'D LEARN

shut. Can you say fire hazard? Can you say foreigner dies of smoke inhalation trying to claw her way out of a locked building? Can you say Dante would have used this as an example of a level of hell if he'd known about it? I tried not to be a jerky foreigner who needed to control everything, so (logically) I set up an appointment with the school officials to discuss options. The clearest and easiest solution was (obviously) to give us a key so that in case of a fire we could let ourselves out.

However, this was not an obvious solution to all. The school officials assured me that I did not need to worry because in case of a fire, the person assigned to sleep in the small room by the front desk would unlock the door. (These were intelligent people; surely they understood the nature of smoke inhalation.) I tried coming at the subject from another angle, but when that did not work, I left the meeting assured.

Assured that if a fire started, I would die. Sigh. All for the cause of Christ, right?

The school walls and the guesthouse chains became symbolic for me. What is stressful for one person can be comforting to another. Neither the walls nor the chains were going to change, and I was the outsider. I needed to find a way to manage the stress in a way that did not eat me up on the inside or come out sideways in snarky, unloving ways.

You too have two types of behavior: who you are when you are secure and who you are when you are stressed. Also like me, you might not know what will cause you stress in your first year because you will be in situations you have never been in before. I did not know that I would be living in a walled campus or being chained in every night. Neither was mentioned in the school handbook I received before I moved to China, but even if they had been, I am guessing I would have found them endearing and all part of living in another culture.

Learning to understand if you are speaking from stress or security is invaluable as you adjust to life on the field. So much will be new this year, and as we discussed earlier, you might see new sides of yourself. Several survey responses touched on this point:

"I was a really good language learner. But I also sadly realized that I was not a nice person to those around me when our stress levels were high. I didn't want to accept that my responses were my fault and that I needed to find healthier ways to deal with the high stress."

"In that first year I learned that I could survive away from family and outside of Australia without all the usual supports. I also learned how selfish I could be and hard to get on with under stress."

"Really the hardest part was that the traumatic violent events occurred so frequently. But a close second was my own poorly understood stress responses, as well as simple immaturity. Perhaps the third hardest thing was my stress responses within a team environment, though I must add that they were also a source of great encouragement too."

To be clear, I am not talking about minimizing significant traumatic events and calling them "stressful." For instance, one survey participant shared, "We ended up getting evacuated and were unable to return to our field of service. It was stressful, traumatic, and very sad." The type of stress she experienced is quite different from living with the school walls I lived with—I get that. Some of you are serving in areas that are extreme in regard to suffering and trauma; we will address them in the next language. For this sublanguage of learning to speak and treat others kindly when in stress, you will need to be aware of when you are stressed so that you can respond in love.

Because each one of us is different, signs that you, a teammate, or a loved one is stressed will vary. WebMD shares the following symptoms of stress:[36]

Emotional symptoms
- Becoming easily agitated, frustrated, and moody
- Feeling overwhelmed, like you are losing control or need to take control
- Having difficulty relaxing and quieting your mind
- Feeling bad about yourself, lonely, worthless, and depressed
- Avoiding others

Physical symptoms
- Low energy
- Headaches

---

[36] Varnada Karriem-Norwood, MD,"Stress Symptoms," *WebMd*, July 11, 2017, https://www.webmd.com/balance/stress-management/stress-symptoms-effects_of_stress_on_the_body#2.

- Upset stomach, including diarrhea, constipation, and nausea
- Aches, pains, and tense muscles

Chest pain and rapid heartbeat
- Insomnia
- Frequent colds and infections
- Loss of sexual desire and/or ability
- Clenched jaw and grinding teeth

Cognitive symptoms
- Constant worrying
- Racing thoughts
- Forgetfulness and disorganization
- Inability to focus
- Poor judgment
- Being pessimistic or seeing only the negative side

Behavioral symptoms
- Changes in appetite—either not eating or eating too much
- Procrastinating and avoiding responsibilities
- Exhibiting more nervous behaviors

I know that the ways I handle stress will not work for every personality or situation, even though I truly believe you would have fun with me in a Zumba class at the gym even if we are the gangly foreigners in the back. Or surely you would find listening to the Denver Broncos through the Internet relaxing. No? At two o'clock on a Friday afternoon

I asked my Facebook friends who live or had lived overseas what helped them deal with stress.[37]

Within seconds, answers started to pour in. I did not expect to have eighty-four responses within a few hours. What became abundantly clear is that finding a way to release your stress on the field is both necessary and unique. As Kathryn said, "Cooking. But that probably stresses other people out! For me, it's a relaxing thing." And the very next comment from Danielle made Kathryn's point when she said, "Chicken nuggets and tater tots . . . it was my go-to comfort meal when life was stressing me out and I just needed something familiar that I didn't have to work so stinking hard to create."

Here are some ideas you could try to see if they help reduce your stress:

"Baths (yes, Jesus loves me, this I know, for my bathtub tells me so), creating (knitting, writing, making things to make our house cozier), time alone, intentional time away with just our family, flowers."

"Intentional rest days to do life-giving things: coffee shop time, reading a book for fun, watching a movie. Permitting myself to relax for specific times daily/weekly."

"Fishing. It is how I recharged my batteries in the US so I found a way and the language to do it in China."

---

[37] You caught me—it was actually at 1:58 p.m. Apparently noting the time I do things is not unique to first-year Amy! Ha-ha!

GETTING STARTED

"When I was in charge of teams, it was good for me to get away for a night or two in another location with fellow believers not with the same organization I was with. I could share and get fresh eyes/ears on a situation."

"I found dropping cheap teacups on my concrete porch to be therapeutic. It was an enclosed area, so easy to clean up, and the concrete made for a better crash. Standing on a stool made for even better leverage."

"Coloring. Using a bullet journal. Buying fresh flowers. Getting my house cleaned. Allowing myself permission to not get massages, even though they are cheap and most people love them, because invariably the masseuse asks my I'm so fat and gives advice on weight loss, and I have a hard time letting those comments slide off from me. So for me, massage ends up causing more stress. Knowing yourself is the point, not everything works for everyone."

"What always helps me is taking some time to talk out the stress with someone and identify the core of the stress and where it is actually stemming from. Most times, if I am overwhelmed, I will just withdraw to escape the stress, but that only distracts me from the stress for a few hours at most. If I take the time to reflect/journal by myself or talk with a trusted friend about how I am feeling and put in the emotional energy to identify its core, the stress is worked through and remedied for the longer term, rather than just subverted for the short term!"

"Running, and watching the Ravens (when they win—when they lose, it usually has the opposite effect, but I'm getting better at managing that, wink)." (I invite you to be a Broncos fan because that is never stressful. Ha-ha.)

"When we had no air-conditioning in our village house, we'd get in our air-conditioned car and just drive. It got us out of the village and helped us cool off."

"Thinking through answered prayers and taking a minute to write them down helped me see our impact. Venting, usually to my husband but sometimes a teammate

"Exploring! A new part of town, a museum, theatre, whatever. Taking my camera along and capturing the beauty. Spoken like a true city girl, right?"

If you ignore your stress, eventually you will explode or implode. Instead, as you can tell from so many responses, you need rhythms to release stress that are daily, weekly, and seasonal. Elizabeth sums up the importance of this sublanguage as "letting myself do absolutely nothing for an hour (or sometimes even a whole day) without guilt. Choosing to tell myself it's okay to spend some time reading a fun book, watching TV, napping, whatever, without feeling like I need to accomplish something at the end of it and without feeling it has to be 'spiritual' in some way. Sometimes my brain and my heart just needed a break from output." So true. The more you learn to live an integrated life and handle your stress well, the more you will move toward God and people

GETTING STARTED

instead of reacting in ways that hurt relationships.

The Parsing of Suffering

It did not take long for me to record in my journal the suffering I saw. On day three in Chengdu I wrote, "Erin and I took our first bus by ourselves! We went exploring trying to find a department store. I have never seen so many beggars in China as I saw downtown. Little kids, a deformed boy with a stomach protrusion, and a man lying on the ground—he reminded me of biblical times. It was distressing to see."[38]

Of all the sublanguages discussed in this chapter, this could turn into an academic discussion of a theology of suffering. But you are going to experience it on a personal level and academic thoughts are not what you need. During this year, most likely you will experience suffering—historical events, natural disasters, or personal tragedy—in ways you could not imagine before you went to the field.

In my first year I taught English to adults. It was the mid-1990s, so that meant my students had been children during the Cultural Revolution in China, one of the most tumultuous eras in modern history. I taught writing and assigned weekly practice writing in their journals. I often chose topics that would help me learn about their lives and culture. I don't remember the topic, but I remember the week several of them wrote about the guilt they felt over being alive and having this wonderful opportunity to study. When they

---

[38] I had spent two summers in China, so though this was my first time to live in China for an extended period, it was not my first time to China.

were children, their parents did not have enough food to feed all of their children. Like King David I wondered, "Why do You stand afar off, O LORD? Why do you hide Yourself in times of trouble?" (Psalm 10:1 NASB).

Since asking my Facebook friends enhanced the section on dealing with stress, I asked for their help on this section as well. While fewer people commented, the comments were longer and heartfelt. In addition, a handful of people private messaged me because what they had to share touched on a deep part of themselves and their stories.

The comments and messages reminded me that you will be exposed to two types of suffering, your own and the suffering of others. It can be complicated if your pre-field training does not address the subject. Ruth (not her real name) wrote, "We saw a young toddler enduring corporal punishment and we had experiences with our own children that in our home culture would be seen as abuse. Although corporal punishment was prevalent where we were living, we were not told that our child might be exposed to it; and when we brought up the subject with field staff and asked why no one had mentioned it, they had no good answer."

People also reported suffering from illnesses (sometimes going on for months), being physically attacked at knifepoint, robbed, cheated, lied to, and nearly dying from inadequate medical services when surgery was needed.

One person recalled being attacked:

"I woke up around 3:00 a.m. with a man hovering over me. He had a stocking pulled over his head and jumped on me and started choking me. I acted as though I had passed out and he tried to tie my hands. I knew I couldn't let him tie me up. I began to pray aloud, and in the Spirit I gained some strength from the Almighty and got my legs under him somehow and kicked him off. I screamed and chased him, but he jumped from landing to landing in the stairwell and scaled the gate. That whole incident was a lesson in God's power to save. I was so aware of His presence, but I still had to work through a lot of fear after that."

"Why do you stand afar off, O LORD? Why do you hide Yourself in times of trouble?" Others in the survey and on Facebook recalled similar experiences:

"As a small part of my job, I taught a couple hours of English each week. At one point, a student told me, 'I am happy when you are teaching.' She had been in a devastating earthquake and was suffering from PTSD/depression. To have even a small hand in helping her find joy again was a privilege."

"The hardest part of my first year was that there was so much suffering and death in my medical ministry."
"Suffering and violence and evil are rampant where I live."

"Living in a place of incredible suffering, especially for women, made me angry at God. This was a confusing place to be—angry at God? How could a cross-cultural worker be that way?!"

If you are not able to ask the honest, hard questions, you will be forced either to stuff and deny what is going on inside of you or risk losing your faith. As one person said, "I can't help you, Amy. Seeing the suffering shattered and destroyed and completely shifted my faith." Your faith will shift as you are impacted by what you see and experience. May God protect your faith in Him.

I was awake in the middle of the night, thinking of this subject and of the comments my friends had written on Facebook. The topic of suffering is pervasive, and this is but one small section of a book. God reminded me that you are in your first year and that learning the language of suffering will take a lifetime. You (and I) do not need to worry that you become fluent in it this year. Instead, as you adjust to your new home and culture, when it comes to suffering, remember these three guidelines:

1. **Lean in and listen**. Often when others around you are suffering, you will want to do something, which is noble and good and godly. But before you can do anything, have a posture of presence and of listening. If there is something you can do, like take someone to the doctor, of course do that! For other, more systemic instances of suffering you will encounter, use this year to ask questions, to learn, and not to come in as an outside "savior." Don't underestimate the power of bearing witness.

2. **Be willing to be uncomfortable**. Suffering makes us uncomfortable, and it should. Allow suffering to do its work. Let it make you feel angry, hopeless, helpless, confused, overwhelmed, or sad. Even as I write these words, I myself want to move through those feelings

quickly by saying something along the lines of "because by feeling those feelings you will move past them." And I do believe that in time you will, but I also believe that you may simply feel helpless for a long time. As someone from the United States I notice within myself how I like to alleviate situations that make me feel uncomfortable by trying to explain them, justify them, see the silver lining in them, or rush to God's provision. There is a time and place for all of those responses. This year, before you jump to them, focus on growing your capacity and willingness to remain uncomfortable.

3. **Know yourself**. Not everyone is wired the same way, and what may be crushing to one may be tolerable to another. This is not a value statement. If God has given you a sensitive spirit, understand that you may need to be mindful of the influence suffering is having on you this year. Honor that God has made you sensitive, and find ways to process what you have seen so you do not carry all the feelings you are having. If you are able to be around suffering and it does not affect you as much as it does others, find ways to serve your family or teammates in this area. If the beggars are out more at the market, consider buying the vegetables more often than others on your team do. Become creative in how you can use your wiring to serve others.

In addition to these guidelines, here are suggestions from people who have gone before you on how to deal practically with the suffering you will see:

"Just this past weekend watching a video I had taken of the view of the slum outside my window, and it still distresses me. But I think it is important not to turn it into a 'why am I so fortunate and they are so wretched?' kind of mentality; instead, learn to identify with those who are in the midst of it. Be humbled by the humility, resilience, and strength of those who have gone through such suffering. Live life with them and create relationships—don't just let it be a high philosophical question that is never engaged with in reality or that we shield ourselves from."

"One place we lived was close to the village funeral home, and the path to the mountain burial plots went right behind our apartments. Several funerals per week broke me and motivated me at the same time. I'd hear those horns start marking the beginning of a funeral, and the tears would start to flow. I found myself moved to pray out loud for those involved in the procession and others affected, and then my prayers would often turn to others I was working with. Remembering that Jesus's compassion so far exceeds our compassion helped. Journaling and writing poetry also helped me process so much of what was going on around me."

"I have three suggestions. First, slow and careful study of suffering in the Bible. My husband and I spent about six months in 1 Peter. It wasn't the first time we had studied it, but different truth and application caught our attention because of our context. Second, books like *Suffering and the Sovereignty of God* or *Where's God When it Hurts?* helped me. Three, because it is overwhelming, not clicking all the urgent news headlines of all the horrible things happening in the world. Compassion fatigue makes it easy to be self-centered about suffering."

"We, like many, have Roma—a marginalized group around here with a generally bad rep—trash divers. We separate the stuff they may want and leave it at the top of the bin or in bags next to it, for instance, piles of cardboard, plastic bottles, or old clothes. Some locals do this too but not many, so we've been encouraging others to do so. We also speak to Roma trash divers and have been known to keep back food and drinks to share. It gives them dignity and shows we take their work seriously. Equally we walk round 'their part' of the market with an open mind. The beggars who use deliberately dirty infants still floor me every.single.time, though."

Ah, the complexities of the suffering you will encounter. To end our time with the subject, I want to pray this verse from Isaiah 43:2 over you: "When you pass through the waters, [God] will be with you; and when you pass through the rivers, they will not sweep over you. When you walk through the fire, you will not be burned; the flames will not set you ablaze."
Amen.

Becoming Multilingual

One of the fun parts of living in a new culture is learning new words that describe something so perfectly it becomes a part of your vocabulary no matter what language you are speaking. Forever I will love the word (the concept really) of *mafan*. The English translation is "hassle," but that is a poor approximation of a word with the depth and beauty as *mafan* has. My teammates and I started to sprinkle words like *mafan* into our conversations.

Can you imagine how off balance you would be if you only spoke grief and never celebrated? Or only spoke celebration and ignored stress and suffering? It is messy and maddening, and necessary, to create space to practice the sublanguages of an integrated cross-cultural life. But ultimately, switching back-and-forth is an honest, life-giving reflection of your call. Begin to cultivate the habits of a language learner in each of these sublanguages, and over time, you might find yourself celebrating, lamenting, relieving stress, and honoring the suffering you see . . . all in the same discussion.

9
Culture and Team (Finally!)

It was an unexciting, ordinary Tuesday afternoon. I walked through the campus and out the front gate to buy butter at a small bakery for baking I was planning to do with my students. Butter was hard to find in the city, with the only store option being tins of butter from Australia. To our delight, we learned we could buy a bag of butter at the local bakery. I learned how to say, "I would like a *jin* of butter," which is roughly a pound, a unit of measure I was familiar with—one less thing to learn, whew. An employee in the back of the bakery took a flimsy blue plastic bag and scooped a *jin* of butter into it and brought it to the front counter. I handed over sixteen *kuai* as I was given my *jin* of *huang you*. Happily I headed home, proud of myself and all the successful learning the little bag of butter represented. On almost a daily basis I would say to myself, "Amy, you are in China! China!" While it was exciting to learn how to order butter, bake in our toaster oven, and boil water to wash dishes, it was also exhausting.

We have talked about how much time ordinary, daily tasks take, but it bears repeating. This year when you get to the end of a day, a week, or a month and wonder what

GETTING STARTED

you accomplished, remember the two E's of learning a new culture: life on the field is exciting and exhausting. Embrace both by celebrating the mundane of daily life and honoring the exhausting parts. Life is not one rolling celebration, and parts will be more tiring than they were back home. Be kind to yourself. Be honoring of the adjustment.

When I asked in the survey for people to share three highlights from the year, no surprise often people shared cultural moments:

"I now have a full heart for the world—I firmly believe that people should live in another culture or country for at least six months. It has opened my eyes and given me such a different perspective on so many things."

"Spending the day at my language nurturer's farm is one of my highlights. It was harvest time for her crops of maize, and even though we had visited this farm together many times, this day felt special. We walked the many kilometers to the farm in the early hours of the morning. Once we got there we spent the next five hours ripping ears of maize of huge stalks and throwing them in a pile. Others joined us and our conversation flowed as we shared the blisters, sweat, and joy of gathering the food that would be my friend's staple for the next year."

"Gaining a local friend all on my own. She gave me a place of fun and helped me feel as though maybe I could belong here. She asked me to be her bridesmaid at her wedding that first year and her wedding was a huge highlight. Also, the

CULTURE AND TEAM (FINALLY!)

first time I actually held a conversation in the local language! I will never take for granted communication again!"

"A highlight was starting to adjust to the language and the culture, discovering that I could go literally anywhere—even to the most dangerous slums in Rio—and God was still with me."

"My three highlights include: 1) Developing a wonderful relationship with the indigenous pastor and his wife that would become a lifelong relationship; 2) Seeing our three-year-old son adjust so easily to the culture; 3) Feeling that despite language errors and cultural slips, we were mostly accepted and appreciated by the people we were serving."

"One of the highlights was befriending our national school business manager and his wife and starting an annual Christmas tradition—which then grew into a monthly date—of going out for a local meal at a restaurant he used to manage. We laughed so much during those times and I learned much about the local culture as well."

"Spending Christmas in Bethlehem where Jesus was born was AMAZING. So far beyond anything I'd ever imagined I'd get to do! I'll never forget standing in the dark in the shepherd's field looking up at the stars and reflecting on the gift Jesus gave in coming to Earth. And the carol service made up of Italians, South Africans, and our small group of Americans singing carols as we celebrated the incarnation. That was COOL!"

Culture Shock

But not all parts of your cultural adjustment will be cool. My friend, Joann Pittman, is one of the premier cross-cultural trainers of our age. When I asked her what advice she would give to those who experience culture shock in their first year, she shared these "7 Things to Know About Culture Shock" with the Velvet Ashes Community:[39]

> I may not be an expert at culture shock (who wants to claim THAT title?), but I've certainly had lots of experience. Here are seven important things about culture shock that I have learned along the way:
>
> 1. The term was coined by Cora DuBois in 1951, but popularized by Kalvero Oberg in 1954. Workers who served overseas before that no doubt experienced all that we now call "culture shock," but they just didn't have a fancy word for it. Maybe they just used the word "hard." I asked my mom, who began serving in Pakistan in 1956, if she or my dad or her coworkers had ever heard of that term when they went. "Nope," she said.
>
> 2. There are typically four stages of culture shock: 1) "Yippee! I'm here." 2) "Whatever was I thinking?" 3) "I can do this." 4) "It's beginning to feel like home."

---

[39] Joann Pittman, "7 Things to Know About Culture Shock," *Velvet Ashes*, August 15, 2014, https://velvetashes.com/7-things-to-know-about-culture-shock.

3. Each person cycles through and experiences those stages at different rates and duration. This can be especially complicated when spouses or children or teammates are at different points in the adjustment cycle than you. I remember a teammate in my first year in China (1984) who was furious with me because I was still in the "Yippee!" phase while she had already crashed into "Whatever was I thinking?" "This [cultural difference] doesn't bother you, and that makes me mad!" she said as she stormed out of my room.

4. It's about the rules. You are in a new place that has a completely different set of rules. Your rules from "back home" don't apply, and you don't (yet) know the new rules. What makes this so alienating is that these rules are the basic stuff of life—how to eat, how to communicate, how to get things done. Sometimes the unfamiliar rules have to do with the role you are playing (teacher, doctor, student, preacher). As Don Larson, my mentor in this area, used to say, "Learn the rules to play the roles." Good advice, I've always thought.

5. There isn't a point at which you ever say, "There! Done!" Remember those cycles? Well, they go round and round and round. This means that if you have been in a place for years and years, you can still experience the confusion and alienation (and even disgust). Culture shock is a part of cultural adjustment, and that is a forever endeavor.

6. Learning the language can mitigate the effects of culture shock. There are few things that can make a person feel more alienated than not being able to communicate with those around her (or him). So it stands to reason that learning the language—learning how to communicate—is a big help. It allows you to enter their world and learn how they understand and process reality. It allows you to learn the rules, and to communicate to the locals who you are. This is incredibly freeing.

7. Learning the language can exacerbate the effects of culture shock. As you learn the language, you encounter the deep structures of the culture—the values and the beliefs about right and wrong. In some cases, this can make things more difficult as you encounter values and beliefs that are diametrically opposed to yours. Adjusting to different eating utensils is one thing; adjusting to looser understandings of truth and justice is another thing.

More Than Two E's

For the most part I loved my new life in China. I loved the smells. Well, most of them. Honestly, I hadn't smelled that much urine in my life, but it was all part of this grand adventure of sharing the hope we have, right?! And if it took me a moment to adjust to flies swarming the meat in the open markets, God was bigger than flies! My journal and letters home are punctuated with so many exclamations, you might confuse me for a junior high girl instead of a grown woman. But I did not know how to convey my joy—"The gal who develops our photos had a note written for me when I picked

CULTURE AND TEAM (FINALLY!)

up my pictures. The kindness I am shown every day blows my mind!!!"—and occasional annoyance—"I had to pay an entrance fee of 50 *kuai* when my students only had to pay two! Really?! Does that seem fair?!!"—other than through punctuation. Cultural adjustment is often like riding a teeter-totter of emotions. Elated, enjoying, embarrassed, enchanted, enthused, edgy, eager, excited, envious, emboldened, enraged, exuberant, exhausted, enamored, ecstatic, exasperated, euphoric, enabled, empowered, and enough.

Up one moment and, without warning, down the next. Yet notice that there are more positive E words than negative. Though cultural adjustment may resemble a teeter-totter, don't take the analogy too far. As Paul reminded us, love does not keep a record of wrong but delights in what is good. Love protects, trusts, hopes, and perseveres (1 Corinthians 13:4–8). That is my prayer for you and my blessing over you as you adjust.

> May God protect your love for the culture you now call home.
> May you trust God to keep your heart soft toward the parts of the culture that confuse you.
> May God guard the flame of hope this entire year.
> May God give you the strength to persevere as you adjust to all the new.
> May this refrain come to mind often: *Love never fails.*
> Amen.

Unhappy in Your Own Way

I would bet good money you have heard that the number one reason people leave the field is because of conflict with other cross-cultural workers. Sad, but true.[40] Thankfully, that is not the only story. Though it is true that in the survey people referenced team dynamics being one of the hardest parts of their first year, others shared that it was the highlight of their first year.

Out of the 184 survey participants, forty-five mentioned team when asked what the hardest part of their first year was:

"We struggled to fit into our team, our leadership was poor, but connection with locals was good."

"It started great, but soon by the end of the first year, miscommunication with teammates began to happen."

"Four months into our first year we were relocated to another field. It was in the same country, but a five-hour flight away and very different work from the city we had been planning to serve in. This was unexpected to us, but we eventually learned that our senior leadership had been leaning toward closing the work in our city before we even got there. This led to a lot of hurt and mistrust toward our sending organization and teammates who had not told us about the problems we were walking into."

"Team, team, team. And I'm on a relatively healthy team filled with people I get along so well with relationally. But

---

[40] Carlton Vandagriff gives five reasons in addition to conflict as to why a cross-cultural worker might leave the field prematurely: excitement without calling, spiritual immaturity, poor health, children's needs, and sexual sin. You can read more here: https://www.imb.org/2017/09/28/5-things-keep-people-off-mission-field/.

I was not prepared for what life is like living on field with several other families who all have a say in each other's finances, ministry, and how we spend our time each day. I am so grateful I get to do this life with team (so, so thankful), but it's challenging!"

"Constant team changes. I was part of the first part of a pioneer team that was sent out, so for the first six months we had new team members arriving. It was part of my duty to orient them to the city—all while still being very new myself and not really being able to deal with all the changes myself. We also had team conflict happening at the same time."

"Being a remote member of a team and being the only non-US member in a 99 percent US team."

"Understanding and communicating with teammates who had issues before we arrived."

"Lack of support from my mission agency and team on the field. Seriously, they didn't meet us at the airport and we didn't speak the language, so that was incredibly disappointing and hard. I arrived without any knowledge of how or where to change money in a country where no one spoke English. They explained that no one was there to meet them when they arrived, so they thought it a good 'test' for the newcomer. Advance notice of this lack of team attitude would have been helpful!"

"I ended up with team leaders who think and operate

completely contrary to my natural tendencies, and it was so, so hard to navigate that. It took years to heal some wounds and truly forgive them for some things that happened."

"Community life was hard. Living on a logistical base with 40–150 people, depending on the season, brought more challenges than I expected, especially since I had lived there the year before during my training."

Reading through these answers reminds me of *Anna Karenina*'s opening line: "Happy families are all alike; every unhappy family is unhappy in its own way."[41] Happy teams are also alike, and every unhappy team is unhappy in its own way. I was saddened as I read these responses, but we need to be honest about the reality that team life can be challenging.

The Role of Belonging in Happy Teams

While it is true that some teams are awful, unhealthy, disappointing, or just hard in the normal way that relationships are hard, we can also rejoice that some teams are happy, healthy, and a source of deep support and friendship. Here is how some of the survey participants described their time with team:

"I loved loved loved my expat community. God taught me a lot about intentional community before I moved overseas, and I really tried to be as open and willing to do community as I could here. I have been blessed with good friends that I

---

41 Leo Tolstoy, *Anna Karenina*, (New York: The Penguin Group, 2000), 1.

call family even after just a year and a half."

"I had an amazing team. I had been in communication with some of them for at least a year before I arrived, so I landed feeling like I already had friends here. They helped me, supported me, and encouraged me, and I know it made all the difference in giving me such a positive first-year experience."

"I learned that the body of Christ comes from so many different backgrounds and we can all lean into team and learn how to get along."

"We intentionally built a good bond together and made time for each other and team. We laughed and shared heartaches together: tears of laughter, tears of sorrow, and the wide range in between."

"The Lord's faithfulness in the midst of so much hardship and my team really coming around me and supporting me in hard times."

"At the tail end of the year, after a counseling class, my roommate/team leader and I had a knockout, drag-down fight (just verbal) that honestly finally helped us get stuff on the table for us to discuss and become close friends."

"A highlight was being cared for by the team as a newbie on my birthday."

"Building close relationships with teammates. We worked

together, explored Portugal together, and spent a lot of evenings hanging out after work."

What comes through is the way that people belonged *to* and *in* their teams. God wants us to belong—to Him, to each other, and to ourselves. But belonging, true belonging, takes work. Paul talked about belonging in his letter to the Corinthians: "God's various gifts are handed out everywhere; but they all originate in God's Spirit. God's various ministries are carried out everywhere; but they all originate in God's Spirit. God's various expressions of power are in action everywhere; but God himself is behind it all. Each person is given something to do that shows who God is" (1 Corinthians 12:4–7 MSG). This passage sounds kumbaya-ish. Read by itself, it is. But when you look at the broader context, you see that Paul is not talking about holding hands and humming together. He is talking about both the *importance* of belonging to something bigger than ourselves and the *challenge* of belonging to something bigger than ourselves.

In chapter 12 of Corinthians, Paul lays the groundwork for needing variety in the body. He spends considerable space laying the foundation because chapter 14 tells us that the Corinthians did not value all the gifts equally. Those who had the gift of prophecy and speaking in tongues were considered better than those who had been given gifts such as healing, helping, or guidance. To truly belong, a Corinthian needed to prophesy, speak in tongues, or exhibit both of these gifts. The rest of the gifts were fine, but the really cool cats had one of these two gifts. Just like for the Corinthians, ranking and comparison are at the root of many team problems. Between chapters 12 and 14 comes one of the most quoted passages in the Bible, the well-known description of love. The passage is referenced so often, we even discussed it earlier. If you didn't know better, Paul's interjection about love in the midst of serving together could feel off topic. But you and I know he is right on point. Love and belonging are woven together.

In the short run, ranking is easier than loving. Belonging can be messy, time-consuming, and costly . . . and worth it. Near the end of his letter, Paul reminds the Corinthians that belonging to each other is not merely for their own personal enjoyment; it blesses and honors God as well. He said, "Therefore, my dear brothers and sisters, stand firm. Let nothing move you. Always give yourselves fully to the work of the Lord, because you know that your labor in the Lord is not in vain" (1 Corinthians 15:58).

That is your hope, isn't it? That your labor for the Lord is not in vain. Keep working for belonging on team. Keep resisting ranking because your labor for the Lord is *not* in vain.

A Tale of Two Teams

A Tale of Two Cities begins, "It was the best of times, it was the worst of times, it was the age of wisdom, it was the age of foolishness, it was the epoch of belief, it was the epoch of incredulity, it was the season of Light, it was the season of Darkness, it was the spring of hope, it was the winter of despair."[42] Before writing this chapter I had not noticed the tie-in between classic literature and life on the field. Because

---

42 Charles Dickens, *A Tale of Two Cities*, (New York: Penguin Books, 2003), 1.

GETTING STARTED

both literature and team involve relationships, well-known lines speak volumes.

In the United States I had wonderful coworkers, a great roommate, and supportive supervisors. I was in a small group and on several committees at church and had friends from a variety of outlets. I ate breakfast at home, lunch at work, and dinner here and there. I did not have a daily practice of praying with the same person or small group. Enter my teammate Erin. We had the same job, the same housing, the same boss, the same church, the same social circle; we ate every meal together and prayed together daily together. "It was the epoch of community, it was the epoch of overlap," to riff on Charles Dickens. Team life was like no relationship I had experienced before. It was exciting and exhausting. To this day, I have a bond with Erin—Erin, another E word!—that is special. To help your team represent the "age of wisdom" more than the "age of foolishness," I have six suggestions:

1. **Examine your expectations.** What words do you use to describe your team? Often the word "family" is used, and I have seen more than one first-year cross-cultural worker very frustrated and hurt by their team because the team "wasn't acting like a family!" What they meant was, "This team isn't acting like my family." When you hit bumps, check your expectations; you might need to adjust them. Or you might realize your expectations are reasonable and you need to seek outside counsel.

2. **Invest in your team relations.** I understand that you want to do what you have been called to do, and

CULTURE AND TEAM (FINALLY!)

investing in people who are not your primary relationship might feel like an enormous waste. After Jesus washed the disciples' feet, He said, "A new command I give you: Love one another. As I have loved you, so you must love one another. By this everyone will know that you are my disciples, if you love one another" (John 13:34–35). People will know you are Jesus's disciples not by your amazing language skills or how well-behaved your kids are but by how you treat your teammates. Valuing your teammates and their contributions and abilities will have ripple effects that you may never know.

3. **Clarify your purpose.** Why are you a team? And if the answer is, "Because our organization assigned us to this team," you know that is a weak foundation. Spend time building a stronger foundation by agreeing on why you are a team and what your purpose is.

4. **Celebrate accomplishments and share sufferings.** Strong-knit teams are there for each other and are quick to recognize accomplishments and to share the hard moments as well. Start early in your year with small celebrations and shared suffering to help set the tone for your team.

5. **Develop your skills.** Okay, this first year your goals are to love God, learn to live in your new home, and begin to get your ministry legs. But in the second year, read a book about communication, attend an online workshop for cross-cultural workers, listen to podcasts, keep growing as a person. Over and over it was mentioned in the survey that the reason team was

so hard was because of a lack of interpersonal skills and a need to learn conflict management. Continue to learn about yourself and how to interact well with others.
6. **Ask for help.** If your team needs help, get help. I wish this were not true, but there are some very unhealthy people on the field. As a new person, you bring fresh eyes. If something seems off, find safe, wise people and, out of love for the person, your team, and the work, advocate for a situation to be addressed.

~~~

Many of Paul's letters contain themes related to culture and teams, showing that the issues of navigating culture and interacting with people are not new. This year you may see his letters in a new light as discussions of food, worship, caring for the poor, etc. need to be reexamined in your new context. "One another" is used one hundred times in the New Testament and 60 percent of them by Paul.[43] The phrase echoes through scripture, reminding us that belonging to each other takes work, and is worth it. May two of your greatest joys this year be the culture and the people you serve with.

---

43 Jeffrey Kranz, "All the 'One Another' Commands in the NT [infographic]," *Overview Bible*, March 9, 2014, https://overviewbible.com/one-another-infographic.

Conclusion

One of my favorite Chinese words is *dongxi*—stuff. The literal translation is "east-west," a little of this and a little of that. So much of life on the field is made up of *dongxi*. After a wonderful yet exhausting retreat for cross-cultural workers, we had an afternoon off and I decided to go boogie boarding with other volunteers. We had heard chanting for an hour but did not realize until it was too late that the chanting was for a Hindu funeral. Picture this, we are dressed for the water and began walking on the sidewalk headed for the water. Unexpectedly we passed five burning pyres on our left and a crowd of mourners on our right. The only respectful response was to keep our heads down and walk as quickly as we could. Talk about the heartbreaking randomness of what can happen to you on the field. It is only fitting that a book about your first year does not have a tidy conclusion. Instead, I have four more thoughts that did not fit anywhere else but need to be included.

Stage of Life
Take your stage of life into consideration this year and be kind to yourself. Are you a recent college graduate? Some of your experiences are not only about transitioning to the field but also involve normal life transition to adulthood. Do you have young children? Life is going to look "smaller" than it does

for your teammates and colleagues who do not have young children. Part of your calling is to help your kids adjust to the field on their time schedule. Are you "older" and going into full-time language school? Good for you. However, older brains are not able to learn as quickly as younger brains. Are you an empty nester with college-age or young adult children back home? They still need their mom and dad, so some of your time goes to them.

Here is what I have learned over the years on the field: every stage of life has its own exhaustion. It is exhausting to navigate the dating scene on the field. (It can also feel hopeless.) It is exhausting to be pregnant on the field, compounded by all the decisions that come with having a baby. It is exhausting being a language student, starting a new job, or providing a service. It is exhausting to homeschool, travel, or set up a project. Can we all just cut each other a break and acknowledge that each path has joys and challenges?

Enjoy the Lighter Side

Thanks be to God that everything about life on the field is not heavy, serious, or dripping with meaning! Voltaire sums it up well: "God is a comedian playing to an audience too afraid to laugh." May cross-cultural workers become known for our ability to laugh and join with God in His comedic work. Asked about highlights or what they learned the first year, these responses touch on the lighter side:

"We got a McDonald's exactly one year in. So, it's gonna make the list." (As it should! My city got a McDonald's my fifth year, and it opened four days before my birthday. Our fellowship, all twelve of us, went there for my birthday! Woot, woot!!!)

"Though my kindergartner flunked out of the local school (You lived in our country . . . he threw his shoes and socks just to spite the teachers, Amy!), God redirected us to homeschooling and I LOVE IT!" (Come on, you have got to laugh, and how shocking that must have been to his teachers!)

"I am capable of more than I thought, like putting together a fan on my first night, even though the instructions were in another language and the pictures were unclear." (I can picture this scene in a movie, can't you?)

"I have fond memories of funny moments setting up home with my husband."

Expect the Unexpected
Obviously, I cannot give you specific warnings and tips on what your unexpected thing may be. But I can say that even if you expect some *dongxi*, you may still be surprised by the reality of your *dongxi*. In the survey, unexpectedness was found in these painful places:

"Money didn't materialize, with delays in the little we did have committed. My appendix ruptured, we had no vehicle, and the house was not what we expected."

"The difficulty of finding someone to relate with and share with spiritually and the frequency of how many times I was lied to, by so many people. In addition, seeing the great suffering around me, often indirectly at the hands of the government, and knowing that in most cases there was nothing I could do about it. I guess I could lump several under the general category of injustice."

"Experiencing subtle racism from some of the people because we were white and they were brown. (We had not expected this.)"

Several people referenced working with other expats from different cultures being more challenging than expected:

"My supervisors very British, so adjusting to non-American team culture was challenging in ways I did not anticipate."

"The challenge of working with American teammates (as a Brit) even though we were working in another language—really found it hard working with what I considered simpler English and incorrect grammar/spelling. It was unexpected."

And the list of where the unexpected popped up could go on!

Go Slow
"Go slow" was the number one response when asked, "What would you like to tell your first-year self?"

"Take it slow. Don't be so hard on yourself; take longer to learn the language and step out of your comfort zone and practice with the locals. Make friends."

"You did great. You've got this. Slow down and enjoy the little moments. Jesus will always be this close."

"Slow down. Think long-term, not just day-to-day. The Lord has things for you and the population of people you are serving and doing life with that you could never fathom or ask for, so take some time to slow down and bask in that, to see what God is doing and marvel."

"Slow down!!! Do not be right today, be love. You will not accomplish a plan, so focus on accomplishing love."

"There is no hurry, prepare well for the future, study, get support in place, build a team. 'If you want to go fast, go alone; if you want to go far, go with others.' I was slow to learn these lessons, wish someone had impressed them upon me."

So, "go slow" is a message for your head and your heart. When you think you are not doing enough, *Go slow*. When you fear that language will never come, *Go slow*. When you want to prove yourself valuable to teammates, *Go slow*. God said, "Taste and see that the Lord is good, happy is she who takes refuge in me" (Psalm 34:8, my paraphrase). Take time to taste and see and enjoy. Go slow.

Start Right. Start Again. Start Together.
Firsts are significant and beginnings hold sway. You can have a terrible first year on the field and go on to have a long and wonderful time of service. But just because you can does not mean you can't hope for, aim for, and work with God

for a good first year. In his book *When: The Scientific Secrets of Perfect Timing,* Daniel Pink says this about beginnings:

> Although we can't always determine when we start, we can exert some influence on beginnings—and considerable influence on the consequences of less than ideal ones. The recipe is straightforward. In most endeavors, we should be awake to the power of beginnings and aim to make a strong start. If that fails, we can try and make a fresh start. And if the beginning is beyond our control, we can enlist others to attempt a group start. These are the three principles of successful beginnings: Start right. Start again. Start together.[44]

Start right. Start again. Start together. Words to remember this year. If you are not with an organization, and even if you are, communities like *Global Trellis, Velvet Ashes,* and *A Life Overseas* provide online ways to connect with others who are also starting.

Firsts are special, and this first year on the field will remain with you long after it ends. Welcome to the field, and since this book has been bathed in love, anticipation, and prayer for you, please receive this benediction from Hebrews 13:20–21:

---

44 Daniel Pink, *When: The Scientific Secrets of Perfect Timing* (New York: Riverhead Books, 2018), 89.

CONCLUSION

Now may the God of peace,

who through the blood of the eternal covenant

brought back from the dead our Lord Jesus,

that great Shepherd of the sheep,

equip you with everything good for doing his will,

and may he work in us what is pleasing to him,

through Jesus Christ, to whom be glory for ever and ever.

Amen.

Acknowledgements

I love reading acknowledgments and learning more of the behind-the-scenes on a book. *Getting Started* was born through a comment in a Velvet Ashes small group. Her comment grew and took root in my thoughts. I tried to start on this book, but the words would not come. For months they would not come. While I do not believe in writer's block—I was still able to write blog posts, emails, and newsletters—I do believe in God's timing. And then a few things shifted in my life and *Getting Started*'s time arrived.

I (foolishly) announced that I would write this book in the month of December. Wanting to gather as many stories and experiences as possible, as you know if you've read the book, I created a survey. Thanks to wonderful online communities like *Velvet Ashes* and *A Life Overseas*, 184 people generously shared their first-year stories. Thank you, thank you, thank you to every one of the 184 who took the survey, without you, *Getting Started* could not be what it is.

Because writing is a solitary activity, in my case done mostly at the public library, in the basement, on the back deck, I am grateful for the writing communities that cheer me on, hold me accountable, and understand that showing up day after day is the real work of genius. Thank you to David Rupert and *The Writers on the Rock* community in Colorado; you were there for me when I showed up saying

GETTING STARTED

I could not write this book and you were there for me when the words flowed. To *The Inkwell* (my fellow Wellies!) you cheer me on when I have absurd plans, am frustrated, or need a quick grammar question answered. Thank you. Finally, to the *KB Mastermind Group*, we might be small, but our hour-long skype calls every two weeks do more to keep me accountable to my goals than anything else I do. Britta Lafont, Esther Wodrich, and Kathy Strong, I love you and a million thanks.

To the readers of The Messy Middle Monthly Letters, you walked through this project with me month-by-month! When I announced this book would be done in a month and then had to come back month after month and tell you that time optimism had bitten me in the behind . . . again(!), you cheered me on and shared how your time optimism was playing out. Letter writing has always been one of my favorite forms of communicating and I'm glad you enjoy letters too.

Books do not happen without many experts investing their time, talents, and wisdom. Every time I asked for help on Facebook, my Facebook friends were quick to reply and help this book move forward. Jonathan Wu suggested the title *Getting Started* on Instagram (Dwight didn't like it, but I loved it!). Leslie Verner, you are the queen of trimming, thank you for believing I could cut 6,000 unnecessary words out of the rough draft. Tanya Marlow and Amy Boucher Pye, you are wordsmith ninjas! Thank you for helping with copywriting and taking my pathetic attempts at the back-cover copy and turning it into the masterful writing it is.

I continue to marvel at the editing process and how

ACKNOWLEDGEMENTS

it parallels the role of the Holy Spirit. Good editors are invested in a book and I am fortunate to have two such editors for *Getting Started*. Stacey Covell, you edited the first four chapters and played a vital role because you have lived and served overseas. You know what it is like to have a first year and assured me that this project had merit. If anyone reading this is looking for an editor, contact Stacey at One Word Editing: www.onewordediting.com. Deb Hall, my beloved editor, once again, I cannot imagine what my writing would be like without you. You are kind, encouraging, but no mere cheerleader, you pointed out where I was not clear, where I was a bit over the edge on snark, and where an example was not, in fact, an example. I have learned more about grammar and clarity in writing from you than from anyone else. Your editing talents are legendary in Colorado. I also highly recommend Deb's editing to you, dear reader. You can reach her at The Write Insight: thewriteinsight.com. I hope you do judge this book by its fantastic cover because Vanessa Mendozzi is a design genius. She can take a few vague ideas I have for a cover and then create a cover that is stunning. Vanessa also did the interior design of the book. She is fast, affordable, and so easy to work with! Contact Vanessa at: www.vanessa-mendozzidesign.com.

I am also grateful for my small group. Tom, Colleen, Becky, Vijay, Dorothy, Mike, Erin, LuAnn, and Jack, thanks for faithfully asking about and praying for this book. You are the best, and I love our times together. Finally, thanks to my family. I remember the year leading up to my first year in China, then letters and phone calls that first year, and how you gathered at the airport with balloons and eagerness to welcome me home. I love you Mom, Dad, Elizabeth, Laura, Del, Sue, Emily, Katy, Anna, and Chloe.

Dear reader, I am also grateful you are here. Thank you for buying *Getting Started*, could I ask one more favor? Would you please help this book to get into the hands of others who need it? Please leave a review on Amazon (it does not need to be five stars, any review helps) and think of one person you can tell about this book. Thank you, thank you.

Amy

About the Author

Amy Young is a writer, speaker, and advocate for embracing the messy middle in life. After nearly twenty years in China, she cofounded the online community Velvet Ashes and founded Global Trellis, which provide spiritual and professional development to cross-cultural workers where they are (no travel needed). Amy also helps cross-cultural workers flourish by regularly blogging for Velvet Ashes, A Life Overseas, and China Source. She enjoys cheering for the Denver Broncos and the Kansas Jayhawks. Though she misses steaming dumplings in Beijing, Amy currently lives in Denver, Colorado and, much to her surprise, enjoys gardening.

Also by Amy Young:

- Looming Transitions: Starting and Finishing Well in Cross-Cultural Service
- Looming Transitions: Twenty-Two Activities for Families in Transition
- Looming Transitions Workbook
- Love, Amy: An Accidental Memoir Told in Newsletters from China
- Enjoying Newsletters: How to Write Christian Communications People Want to Read (Formerly All the News That's Fit to Tell)

Printed in Great Britain
by Amazon